I TOOK THE
RED PILL

NAVIGATING THE RABBIT HOLES
OF A SPIRITUAL AWAKENING

PALLAS

I Took the Red Pill: Navigating the Rabbit Holes of a Spiritual Awakening
Published by Pallas Awakens Publishing, LLC Thornton, Colorado

ISBN: 978-0-578-31251-4
BODY, MIND & SPIRIT / New Thought

Cover and Interior design by Victoria Wolf, wolfdesignandmarketing.com, copyright owned by Pallas.

PALLAS AWAKENS
PUBLISHING

Dedicated to all those with different pieces of knowledge that came before me that allowed me the ability to present this in a cohesive framework for others.

And to you, the reader...for taking a chance and going down a rabbit hole and seeing where it takes you.

CONTENTS

HEALING CHAPTERS

PROLOGUE

A phenomenon has been occurring. I discovered early in my Awakening that I was not alone. Not only were there a lot of people who had already come to certain conclusions that would ultimately be the guides on my path to discovery, but there were also thousands if not millions of people simultaneously going through the same things I was. Like a wave of people, all of a sudden having switches flipped on to the massive, convoluted discovery of truth. Something much larger than living day to day is going on globally. That in itself was both relieving and terrifying. Relieved I wasn't alone and just getting weird and yet terrified by what that might mean.

I went in search of why Universal Laws had failed me. The Law of Attraction, positive intention, and manifestation, beliefs, actions, energy, dreams, etc. It all failed me. So, I decided to turn to unconventional means to figure out why. What I did not expect to discover is a path that led me on a spiritual (not religious) journey that revealed the deception of humankind over the last 13,000 years and how it would connect into my life and others and, even more importantly, why that mattered on a massive scale.

What started as an existential treasure hunt ended in a life-changing transformation of my body, mind. and soul. They call this an Awakening or Dark Night of the Soul (DNOTS). Usually, one experiences this when a significant event that was emotionally charged occurred. Loss, separation, frustration, despair seem to be the keys. When you experience a DNOTS, you cycle the full range of emotions a human being can have. It isn't a beautiful process. It is messy, ugly, terrifying, and horrifying. But in the end, you crack open and grow into something more beautiful than what you were. You understand things differently, see them differently, respond to them differently. What ultimately happened physically, emotionally, and mentally with me during this process, actually has happened to a large number of people too.

The information herein is an accumulation of the input, knowledge and conclusions of many individuals over time and, in some instances, going back for thousands of years. Some of it is proven, some of it is theory, but everything starts as a theory until it is provable. Even some of the biggest mysteries of the universe are still wrapped in theory. Yet how many times has science fiction turned into science fact?

What I found was the experiences in my life made more sense in this new framework of information and thinking. It isn't even my full story. Just a small part of it. I use my story of Awakening and my experiences to lay over the framework of the system at large in telling the real story or the bigger picture so you can understand how everything is connected and why that is important to you. We are all connected, more than you realize. We have power in our interconnections, and we have the ability to heal ourselves. The situations we endure in our lives and the people in them are not by chance, but instead are an extremely organized life experience … that was actually crafted by *you*.

NAVIGATING THE RABBIT HOLES OF A SPIRITUAL AWAKENING

CHAPTER 1

THE PRIMER

The goal of this book is to help guide you down the rabbit holes in your Awakening. While I say this is the guide, it is important to understand that it is simply my journey and what I experienced and learned. But that, hopefully something I write, you can identify with and feel a sense of peace and comfort that you are not alone, you are not going through this alone. There is, in fact, support out there both informationally and emotionally in the community.

All of the topics mentioned in this book give you surface-level information like a summary version, which are meant to give you a piece of information that will help ignite something in you to seek out more knowledge on your own and find what resonates with you.

The word "resonate" is key here. Just because I discuss something that does not resonate with you, doesn't make it right or wrong. It is just the path I have been led down and my gifts and my experiences, and what feels right to me. You have your own gifts and experiences, and they are meant for you to use in a specific way on your life path. You have to tune in to what does resonate with you. In fact, that has been what I have learned the most and why there really isn't a manual or guide; because everyone's journey and experience is different and very personal. We don't all have the same size fits all abilities, and we all have different life paths we are on.

There are traps everywhere in this process, and it is easy to get snagged into some. I help point out some of them to help you, so hopefully, you won't get stuck. I was fortunate to find the mainline pretty quickly, though I had a couple of traps I stepped into but learned to get back on the main path. When I use the word traps, the best I can liken it to is Indiana Jones during The Last Crusade when he goes to step on the J for Jehovah only to fall and immediately realize no, it started with an I. There is misinformation along with these traps, which means you have to use your discernment quite a bit. Everything has been polluted to some degree. I have seen quite a bit where someone had it, then at the end, they took a hard right, and I went no, you lost the plot. I will discuss the main ones I found, so hopefully, you don't get stuck in them.

There are some tough sections to get through on topics because it means leaning into something you never leaned into before. I know—I had to get through them myself and mentally come to an acceptance that these things made more sense and felt more right than the other things I had been told as factual previously by people I had trusted. I also wanted to keep things real, so you can see the depth of darkness I had to come out of to understand how hard it might be for you. But it is possible, and there is a healing aspect to this journey that is important for you to take.

If you are currently going through your Awakening, then this book is for you. It is an experience one goes through that entirely changes their core belief structure. One in which what we have been told to believe is realized to not be the truth. It is an experience where the masculine/ego side of you, essentially dies and in its place, you find a rise of the feminine side that now begins to be in balance. The DNOTS is a journey in reflection of yourself. The owning of experiences you have had has been part of your design in the path to enlightenment of your soul. It exposes the worst of horrors that have occurred in this lifetime (and often past lifetimes), the role you played in them, the emotionally sitting in that headspace, and the healing that comes after coming to terms with it. Sitting in the knowledge that individuals or groups of specific people have not just deceived you your entire life but also have deceived those that you love. It very much is an existential identity crisis that changes you. One in which nothing is as it seems anymore and the discovery of information is something that cannot be undone. Once you know, you cannot unknow it, and there is confusion and horror even in that especially because you didn't realize what you were going to find before you found it.

The experience can often feel like a horrible bout of depression because you have the same kinds of thoughts and feelings one has during depression. It illustrates things we have emotionally held onto things that no longer serve a purpose. As you are energetically lifted into a higher state of consciousness and thought processing/decision making. This process might be days, weeks, months, or years even depending upon the person. Each human that raises the frequency of themselves further contributes to raising the collective consciousness of all souls.

I encourage you not to simply take my word for things, do your own research. Try to see if you can find information that supports these avenues and if you can discredit them. I was not able to discredit them as possibilities.

There is a significant chance, that after reading a bunch of my stuff, you will have lightbulb moments going off for you and all of a sudden things in your past that you just didn't understand or couldn't understand why you couldn't get past or whatever, it all starts to make sense. Dots started connecting everywhere, and to some degree, it is super enlightening and also mind blowing. Kind of like, why did I not put that together until now? Well, in part, because we are taught to think of coincidences and discount them instead of synchronicities and how it all connects.

CHAPTER 2

THE AWAKENING

How did I awaken? When I look back at my mind-shifting experience, I am not sure I was "entirely" asleep. As a strong independent female who always did her own thing, there were concepts over time that I definitely came to my own conclusions on. This was a gradual process brought on by urges I could not resist over a year and a half period. It happened in an unexpected way yet in the way it needed to in order for me to understand it in all its complexity. Every piece of new discovery had me continuing to ask why, or can I prove there is no viability with this piece of information? Everything was building upon itself in layers until I finally got to what seemed like the end. Or the end of what is currently known.

Someone could have sat me down and explained the overarching info on aliens in general in thirty minutes, and I would have been like, yeah, I can get behind that. I've always thought there is no way we are the only complex living organisms in the universe. I've always thought the Earth's timeline with humankind as it was taught to us in school was nonsense as well. I believed we weren't alone, people have seen aliens, been abducted, etc., but I was in no way a conspiracy theorist. Did I trust the government? Of course not. History has shown you should never blindly trust those in power.

Someone could have run down the spirituality of souls' path and the pollution by humankind to religion, and I also would have gotten behind it quickly. I had dropped my religion two decades prior and had never felt better leaving the chains that bind behind. I actually felt a weight lifted off me when I did that. And it is this notion that made me feel like I was never really asleep. There was always some part of me that innately knew better than to blindly accept the information that had been fed to me at face value. Especially over the years when too many belief systems were out there that could not logically be explained.

But it was the psychic plane and different levels of consciousness that blew it all open and then connected it together. I believed in psychic abilities, but not that I had them. I also had this preset belief that if you are psychic, then that was all encompassing. I was so very wrong. What surprised me the most in hindsight is how much scientific evidence and information is out there that supports all three planes. Several famous scientists throughout time have dropped notes that we should incorporate metaphysics into the physics conversation.

About six months after my mother died, I was getting severe urges to see a psychic. Weird things were happening in my house. Lights would flicker, things would move, my electronics were malfunctioning randomly. I would feel something cold against my skin in places at different points in time. I knew it was my mom. I just felt like she was frantically trying to tell me some things from the spirit world. Additionally, circumstances surrounding the lead up to her death made us suspicious of some things.

So we went to a medium. I was open, and everything was resonating. It felt like she was right there saying those things. I had come to terms with my mother's death. She had been a sick woman for years, so for me, her death was knowing she was now at peace and no longer in pain or misery. After the session, less weirdness happened in my house.

Several months went by, and I was severely frustrated by career issues that just felt like I was blocked. It felt like I was standing at a big wall with the doors of opportunity in front of me, and none were opening. Over a three-year period, my desire and belief that I was meant to be a warrior for women on the business front was so unbelievably strong with me that I figured out what I was meant to do. I never before then really felt like I knew what I was supposed to do in life, just that there was something. Like I was on an airport walkway and, occasionally, it would jerk in a direction and be like—okay we are doing this now. But the walkway was leading me somewhere, and I always had hope it would get me to where I eventually needed to be. Hoping the skills, I learned along the way, were leading to something useful.

I was sitting in a place where I had worked for a year and a half on detailed plans for something that I felt was my destiny to do. I dreamed it, envisioned it, believed it, put energy out there corresponding to that to manifest my desire, put actions and working plans behind all of it. I made persistent contact, trying to get anyone to reply to me. The position was available, no one wanted it, and no one seemed to know what to do, which seemed odd because it was so clear to me. Then I waited. And waited.

I got a big middle finger back. Nothing, not even a reply of "thank you for your interest, but we aren't interested." I just didn't understand how I could believe something so implicitly at the core of my being, do the work behind it to manifest my destiny, and then nothing. This wasn't even something that was really self-serving. This was an advancement for women on a global stage. The Law of Attraction … failed. Manifestation … failed. Something was wrong. Something was amiss. I couldn't put my finger on it, but I knew I had to seek out answers in a different way if I was going to figure this out.

I had been fighting this urge to talk to another intuitive (psychic). Something was welling inside of me, and I knew this was the only path that might give me answers. I called up a local psychic, and the two things that bothered me after the reading were that I had The Hanged Man, so I would need to change my perspective on something. Okay I have to change my perspective on something, but what? What perspective did I need to shift? Then there was the Dragon's Lair card, and she noted that I was guarding a treasure fiercely inside me, like a secret I was keeping from the world and not letting anyone see. That I was divinely protected, and this path would challenge me. While the rest of the reading resonated, that one card and that whole bit ate at me. I am a person who has spent a lot of time on herself, knowing herself inside and out, the good, the bad, what we work on, why we work on it, who we want to be. Etc. So this was like … I have a secret about myself that I am not letting out? HAHAHAHA okay whatever. But, I couldn't let it go. What was this secret?

Another couple of months go by, I am still circling around this topic, with no progress. I called another intuitive. Fuck it. Who cares. This is my business if I want to talk to psychics. But it was this one that flat out told me, you are an empath and an intuitive, and you need to read *The Emotion Code*. As if someone had told her to say those specific things to me. I ended that session going, "what does that mean?" So I started looking up empath, and then my mind went through an explosion of understanding from processing everything that came from that realization. Going back in my timeline and reviewing. It took me two weeks to come back and say, wait, what is this intuitive word? Does it mean something different than I originally thought it meant?

When I realized an intuitive was someone with otherwise ESP abilities and that "I" was apparently one of these people ... I laughed and laughed and laughed. Me and gifted abilities. HA. Then I reviewed what the different Clair's were and looked back at my life situations and moments, and then my mind went ... wait a minute ... .

I needed more time to process this realization. Then I definitely spun emotionally all over the map for a few weeks. Being an empath with no control over it on top of having Clair abilities, oh my goodness, not exactly the best place to be mentally, emotionally, or physically. I was vibrating like a honey bee that never stopped working. Then I calmed down. Then I freaked out again cause I realized I have no idea what I am doing, and I have kind of shot myself in the foot in a couple of areas without realizing it. I have intentionally suppressed some of my abilities, but I don't exactly know how I did it, so I don't exactly know how to undo what I originally did. I don't know where to go, who to ask. What this grounding and shielding stuff is and how to do it. Spinning ... out ... of ... control. So confused, so scared, lots of anxiety, lots of tears.

To give you an idea also as to why this idea that I had abilities or could possibly be considered special was so hard for me to believe is because my core belief about myself was that I am not special and I have no real value. Part of my journey on this path is I have had to change my core beliefs about myself that I am, in fact, special and have a boatload of value. As do you.

I struggled for a while with what constituted the term Awake in this process. I found people stuck in the empath and intuitive but clearly hadn't fallen down the hole like I had into the rest of the stuff. People half clinging on to their old belief systems of religion while pretending they had let go 100% into spirituality. People fully in the alien space but not spiritually connecting the two. But what I also saw were so many people being confused. Really confused. And I was right there with them.

Surprised I found all the information as had others, but couldn't find where someone had put this together in a book. I found oodles of books dedicated to each of the topics, but where was the book that gave you the main line in understanding how all this connects? I was being led on this path. A combination of feeling both pushed and pulled.

I would say that being Awake is being consciously aware of the truth that has been hidden from you and realizing your true soul's purpose. To take you through the first part of my journey is to explain more about psychic abilities so you can understand how they are different, do any apply to you and then start running you through, why does it matter, why do we have these abilities? What does it mean? In finding the answers to these questions, I found more questions and the web of the matrix just got bigger and bigger.

CHAPTER 3

ENERGY

I didn't expect this endeavor to have so much science or scientific theory behind it. Certain names would keep popping up in the areas of physics and quantum mechanics. What started as a trip down the metaphysical path, ended me right into energy, light, sound, vibration, and frequency at the cornerstone of it all.

Albert Einstein famously said, "Everything is energy and that's all there is to it. Match the frequency of the reality you want and you cannot help but get that reality. It can be no other way. This is not philosophy, this is physics."

Einstein first discovered zero-point energy. It is the lowest possible energy that a quantum mechanical system can have or otherwise known as the vacuum state, the energy of a system at a temperature of zero. Zero-point energy is vibrational energy that molecules retain even at the absolute zero temperature, and because no object can ever have precise values of velocity and position simultaneously, molecules can never come completely to rest. Those values of velocity are considered vibrations, and every tangible thing on this planet is made of matter. Those particles of matter all vibrate at different frequencies, which allow them to stay together in a tangible form.

Information transfers via energy waves. The astral plane is made of quantum waves, and we tap into those waves. In fact, you can use string theory to explain it. Pathways from the past also connect to the future via this concept, which is why time doesn't really exist. It simply is a human construct.

Nikola Tesla famously said, "If you want to find the secrets of the universe, think in terms of energy, frequency and vibration. The day science begins to study nonphysical phenomena, it will make more progress in one decade than in all the previous centuries of existence."

Who was Nikola Tesla? Only the most important inventor, mechanical and electrical engineer in the last 150 years, who has interestingly been wiped out of most educational books, so no one knows who he is. I had never heard of him before the electric car was named after him and then found him everywhere as I stumbled on this path. In fact, if you look back at the last 2,000 years, undoubtedly, the greatest invention has been the printing press. Everything from communication spawned from that basic invention that launched communication of ideas, imagination, and facts on a mass scale. I would even venture that the internet is the next greatest communication invention, allowing us to connect in real time globally to others.

However, in this process, what I realized is that the greatest invention that had the ability to change the entire landscape of our world was created by Tesla. It was scrapped because investors couldn't or wouldn't make money on it, and Tesla wanted to give the world free and clean energy.

Instead investors decided Edison's way to capitalize on energy worked better for them. I was a capitalist for a long stretch of my life, but by the time I got done with my Awakening, I had shed all of that. Today you are able to have wireless technology and most of it is powered by batteries that are toxic to the environment. Tesla had the beginnings of wireless technology one hundred years ago.

In case you aren't understanding the gravity of this, imagine with renewable natural energy, there is no need for coal, oil, natural gas, or nuclear energy. Imagine how many things we use today that have polluted our air, water, and the Earth. Our oceans would not have been poisoned by oil spills or nuclear disaster leaks. Our air would be breathable all over the world. We wouldn't be contaminating our groundwater with pipelines, wells, and leaks. Your electric bill would be a fraction of what it is today. Let that sink in for a bit, and then understand that Tesla had it figured out about one hundred years ago.

But JP Morgan, Eastman Kodak, and Rockefeller, well, that just wasn't financially in their interests. Fuck the little people, fuck the world. So they did. When you dig into Tesla further, you find that he was also very much into the secrets of metaphysical dimensions. A lot of his work came to him in visions. So all the psychic stuff I reference is also littered with Tesla between metaphysical and scientific theories. Even Sigmund Freud dabbled in metaphysics intertwined with the science of the brain. If you go back and review Einstein's quotes, speeches, and findings, you see that he, too, tries to bridge the gap between the metaphysical and science.

To get an idea of the wealth of inventions that Tesla gave the world, he was kind of like a modern-day Da Vinci. In fact, go back and look at Da Vinci because he pops up a few times as well. He was way ahead of his time—inventions like the tank and helicopter, among other things.

While Tesla held about 278 patents by the time he died, here is a small sample of things that Tesla was responsible for: the radio, rotating magnetic field powered by alternating current (AC), AC motor, Tesla coil, magnifying transmitter, Tesla turbine, shadowgraphs (X-rays), neon lamps, induction motor (used in vacuums, blow dryers, power tools, etc.). Tesla had several of his patents stolen and produced by others, but he was in no financial position to ever fight them. When asked how he felt about this, he replied with, "I don't care that they stole my idea … I care that they don't have any of their own."

Three hours after Tesla died, the US Government entered his hotel room and seized all his papers. His remaining work going under the guise of national security and effectively burying all of his research for outsider knowledge. Since when does the government move that fast on anything? Who owned the hotel he was staying in? Well, it was *The New Yorker,* so you can figure that one out. The more you read about Tesla and the US Government's involvement, the more you realize they erased this information from being taught as part of our history.

What is vibration? Vibration is a motion of particles in opposite directions when an object's equilibrium has been disturbed. All matter has a vibrational rate. The universe has no solidity. Therefore, the universe and everything that comprises it is pure vibratory energy manifesting itself in different forms.

What is a frequency? Frequency is the rate at which something occurs or is repeated over a period of time. Think of it like your car radio. Receiving broadcasting from multiple frequencies/signals but only tuning in to one of the frequencies then translated as a channel. Just because you are tuned into one frequency doesn't mean other frequencies you can't see or hear don't exist.

Even the planets in our solar system vibrate and emit certain frequencies. Look into some of the videos of the sounds the different planets make. NASA has them, or you can find some on YouTube. Some are rather eerie to listen to, but all the planets emit sound frequencies.

We know that humans are bio-electrical beings. While we are primarily composed of water, we operate with electrical circuitry to make the bodywork. We know the Earth has an ionosphere or a toroidal field. We know the human body does as well. I discuss grounding principles in the Healing Chapters, but when you understand that the Earth is a living thing just as we are, things start to synchronize. Humans are living things, and energy flows through us. Everything vibrates at a different consistency and frequency, along with gravitational pull. Humans are supposed to be energetically symbiotic with the Earth—we weren't meant to destroy it.

Now to add to this. Let's think of energy in this way.

+ Matter = vibrational frequency.
+ Vibration can be described as frequency.
+ Frequency can be expressed as numbers.
+ Numbers can be perceived and organized as geometric patterns or interpreted into a binary code.

This means, we can reduce anything to some sort of mathematical pattern.

The modern binary number system, the basis for binary code, is a two-digit system capable of doing all math computations was invented by Gottfried Leibniz in 1689. German physicist W.O. Schumann hypothesized in 1952 and confirmed in 1954 that there were measurable electromagnetic waves in the atmosphere that existed in the space between the surface of the Earth and the ionosphere. The ionosphere contains an abundance of electrons, ionized atoms, and molecules that stretches from approximately thirty miles above the surface of the Earth to about 600 miles up at the edge of our atmosphere with space. Electrons are discharged and retained on the surface of the Earth through lightning. The measuring of this electromagnetic activity is called the Schumann Resonance.

There are all sorts of external energies that bombard us, even from external places such as solar sun flares. The Earth has been mapped to vibrate its electromagnetic field at 7.83Hz. Human beings have been mapped to vibrate between 6-8 Hz. Do you see how humans are energetically in alignment with Earth? They also discovered that emotions resonate at different frequencies. The higher the light frequency, the higher you vibrate. Negative emotions vibrate you at the lowest points you can be—more on this in the Healing Chapters.

UNIVERSAL LAWS

There are twelve universal laws. You can read up on them more yourself, but I am confident you have heard of most of them already.

1. The Law of Divine Oneness—everything is connected to everything else
2. The Law of Vibration—everything in the universe vibrates, moves and travels in circular patterns.
3. The Law of Action—everything we put thought to, we must put action behind in order to manifest.
4. The Law of Correspondence—our outer world reflects our inner world therefore we need to accept personal responsibility in our lives.
5. The Law of Cause and Effect—nothing happens by chance outside of The Universal laws. Every thought, word, or action is energy.
6. The Law of Compensation—the abundance and flow that comes to you from the cause and effect and vibration you hold.
7. The Law of Attraction—The energy you emit, is the energy you attract.

8. The Law of Perpetual Transmutation of Energy—we have the power to change our vibrational frequency into higher levels through positive change.
9. The Law of Relativity—What we perceive as the force of gravity arises from the curvature of space and time. Space and time are curved when there is matter, energy, momentum, and gravity.
10. The Law of Polarity—everything is on a continuum and has an opposite. There is no Dark without Light.
11. The Law of Rhythm—everything vibrates at a certain rhythm or frequency.
12. The Law of Gender—everything has masculine and feminine principles, and the key is to find the balance of this polarity within us.

When you look further into these, you realize you already had heard or known about most of them before. But they are also interconnected with everything else in this book.

CHAPTER 4

WHAT IS AN EMPATH?

"**W**hat is WRONG with you?? Why are you SOOOO emotional??? Why are you so sensitive???"

I can't even write that line without getting full-body chills about it. I probably heard either of those lines and sometimes together, maybe a few times a week for years from my parents and other people.

"I don't know!!!" The four- to eighteen-year-old me sobbed ....

What was wrong with me? Because clearly, something was wrong with me, right? I mean, if my parents said something was wrong with me, then clearly they were right. They were the authority. They were the smarter/older/experienced humans. Not to mention you have to obey them (no matter what). The Bible says so, and you have to follow the Bible. Something was wrong with me. Okay, I just need to work on not letting anyone see what is wrong with me. So that is what I did.

For almost as far back as I can remember, I have routinely spontaneously combusted with emotions, tears, shakes, or shivering rolling flashes at some point half the time wondering why I was feeling these emotional sensations and physically feeling those emotions manifesting in an offsetting vibration. What was wrong with me?

Crying is bad, showing emotion, being upset, all bad. So I taught myself. As a child, I found a way to go somewhere like my room to isolate myself from others so I could break down privately. As an adult, I taught myself that when I was in the line at the grocery store, patiently waiting my turn, and then BAM it hits out of nowhere, and the tears start to go, I do a slight tilt down of my head so the tears will go either to the eyeball and not the lid, or toward the corner of my eye, then two seconds later, I do a subtle flick of my head, or turn around like, oh I want to look at this magazine, the tears fly right out without messing up my eyes or my makeup. Or if it isn't just going to be a couple tears, usually I will bend over and act like I am struggling to get something low on a shelf so no one can see my face, and I can subtly reach my other hand up to my face to try and deal with it, while my other hand is the distraction point. The magician misdirection. The worst is when you are with one of your close friends or family, and you get caught. The look in their eyes of both confusion, surprise, fear, and then you look at them and are like … damn it and … I don't know what's wrong, and I don't know how to explain what you see. But instead, you say you are fine and it was just an eyelash.

If you are an empath but didn't know, then you didn't make it through what I just wrote above without having a correlating synchronistic realization about yourself. You just started to have that aha moment. Do you try to avoid large crowds or various social gatherings? You like people, but you don't really like being around them? Do you feel the need to withdraw and isolate? Or feel added social anxiety when you thought you would be fine? An empath feels and absorbs other peoples' emotions via energy transfer. They are like a magnet for other people's emotions. I never understood I was absorbing other people's emotions physically via energy transfer until I read about it.

When the psychic told me I was an empath, I walked away and said to myself, "she is saying I have empathy right?" This was an emotional framework for who I was and had always been fighting against because of what others had said to me. I originally researched a bunch of empath checklists, trying to discredit myself somehow. You are telling me that all this time, there really hasn't been anything wrong with me, and it is not some form of psychotic break? It is a mind-blower moment when you realize your perception just shifted on something but in a way that makes more sense. Then the next step is saying, okay this is what I am. There are a lot of others out there that have these same exact things too?

The basic construct of what empathy happens to be the identification of understanding the emotion someone else is experiencing, based on the concept that we too have had that experience or are going through it and thus understand both the emotional and mental state of mind. As a result of previously experiencing those feelings, we understand the emotions the other person is having in that moment.

Here is where it deviates from the definition or idea that you have otherwise been told. An empath is someone who, via transfer of energy, absorbs another person's emotional energy and feels it as if it is their own. Most people who are walking around as empaths are the ones who have major social anxiety issues and feel better when alone or isolated. Because, the truth is, they just don't understand what the fuck is happening to them. I get it. I was in that space. I am an extroverted/introverted empath. I appear as an extrovert, but in many ways am an introvert, mostly because of my empath traits. I grew up with a mother that kept saying to me, what is wrong with you? Why are you so emotional? So I worked really hard at not being emotional—having these experiences when there was no basis for me to have them. I wasn't upset in those moments, but the feelings that would come over me that I had no answers for that triggered emotional and physical reactions within me were just something I couldn't explain, so I just had to hide it.

When someone is an empath, they can channel the actual emotions. I can watch a really good actress on screen, and I can literally pull her emotions that she was channeling while acting that scene a year ago from the film itself. Like instantly. I can burst into tears in a heartbeat when I personally was not even sad and am like—what the ever-living fuck just happened? So the truth is, we need to be finding our natural empaths and telling them what they are, so they can figure out how they are supposed to use their empath ability as well as help them figure out how to control it for both their best interests and others. I do use the term control very loosely because the truth is, we do need to learn to control it, but not in a way that is to suppress it. If you are an empath, then you were NOT meant to suppress it. You were meant to use it. That is also the crappy thing about being an empath. You are kind of like a spiritual energy vacuum. Both good and bad.

Another ability I have as an empath is to become an immediate mirror. I have always known I behave this way. I just never understood why. What I mean by this is, if someone approaches me calmly to have a dialogue, then I am calm. If someone approaches me verbally or physically aggressive and I was calm, it takes me precisely one second to rise up and mirror the same feelings that another individual is expressing toward me back at them.

Before learning how to center my energy and shift my mental perceptions and handle my emotional triggers differently, as an Aries and a natural rager. I become like the Hulk in an instant, and I am ready to SMASH you either verbally or physically. I become like the terminator in my head. Fuck me? Oh hell no, FUCK YOU. That is me. But it took understanding common traits of an empath and how energy and other people's emotions impacts you in a heightened way, to understand I had been mirroring so much in day to day and had understood yet did not understand exactly why. Now it did. It all made sense why I am the way I am. Why no matter how hard I have tried to change who I am, it just is not possible … because I am an empath. I essentially had been fighting against my nature.

An empath is either operating structured or unstructured. An unstructured empath is one who is unaware they are an empath, and as a result they don't do any of the things they need to do to center themselves and learn to deal with this additional energy bombardment. A structured empath is one who is aware they are an empath, who takes steps to maintain, shield, and center their energy on a consistent basis.

To understand how this truly works is to understand the basic principle of Quantum Mechanics, which is that every thought and emotion resonates at a certain vibrational level. That vibrational level translates into a sound frequency which is typically measured in Hz. Energy in motion is "emotion" and is simply a response to a vibration received from elsewhere. So the feeling that one feels as an empath is that underlying energy in motion from receptors. You feel more strongly because your internal vibrational level is already operating at a higher frequency than many others do.

To add to this, let's add in the topic of one's aura. An aura is a person or living thing's electromagnetic field of energy that encompasses the body. Traditionally, it has been thought that your soul/spirit/consciousness resides inside you, tucked away magically in your tummy or something. But recent thinking is that your spirit actually encapsulates and moves through your physical body; identified as one's aura and energetically resonates at different frequency levels which equate to color, the color translates to areas of strength and weakness (see chakras and sound frequency in the Healing Chapters). From there, energy transfers back and forth to people, places, and things, and the strength of that energy is dependent upon the emotional frequency that energy is moving at. Your physical body is a composition of bio-electrical equipment, so the aura concept shouldn't be too much of a stretch. Not to mention, Kirlian Photography has shown that living things give off different color frequencies.

THE DIFFERENT TYPES OF EMPATHS

Note that you can be one type of empath, or several. There are lots of checklists on empaths online that you can search and review and take to see what you identify with.

Emotional—this is the primary one, where it is human to humans, and you feel their actual emotions they are experiencing as if they are your own. Essentially you become a mirror to what they feel. Human emotions have actually been mapped out to energetically resonate at specific sound frequencies that they transmit outward. Note an emotional empath does not need to physically be in the space of others to feel someone else's energy.

Physical—you absorb the energy of those emotions as you are in the physical capacity of that person. I would think that most emotional empaths are also physical empaths, but just in case someone wants a further distinction.

Animal—these are the people who don't just love animals, they identify with them on some level. They are the ones that you feel are extra affected by bad things done to animals. Now, I am not an animal empath. But, I can feel the human who is an animal empath. I can feel the emotions and feelings they are feeling, which is coming from what they feel for the animal. Trippy eh? Many animal empaths can even communicate with animals on a certain level.

Nature—A nature empath is someone who feels pain for living things around us that are being destroyed or damaged. They are the ones that just want to be outside somewhere in nature whenever they can. Nature empaths are also our environmental activists. They are the ones who feel so deeply about the injustice and pain of what we are doing to the environment. Activism doesn't have to be on a grand or loud scale. It simply can be saying, I am going to live my life a certain way while I am here on this Earth because I believe that is the best thing to do and the best way for me to live my authentic life by doing my part to preserve this beautiful place. Often animal and nature empaths feel both but one more strongly than another.

Medical—a medical empath is one who can literally mimic the same feeling in their body as you have in yours. So if your knee hurts, a medical empath whose knee is totally fine will all of a sudden feel their knee hurting as well. You can mirror symptoms of those you love due to the strength of your energy ties. You can mirror someone in front of you or someone else not in your space.

Global—these empaths feel horrific surges in great tragedy. Things that rock the world. These empaths feel the pain on a global interconnected level. They are often fine for periods of time as long as they are also not emotional empaths on top. I read a story of a woman who gave birth on 9/11, and she said when her daughter was born, she screamed for twelve hours straight. We are all connected through light, energy, sound, and consciousness.

As I ran through these and identified that I was an emotional/physical empath, I did my first set of timeline reviews in this process. The trigger phrases were, why are you so emotional and what is wrong with you? It was a massive ball of confusion and relief. That there was this construct at an emotional level that had been identified, and it was normal, and a lot of other people had the same emotional experiences as I had. That I wasn't crazy. Things did happened to me. I felt like a weight had been lifted off me and the *something is wrong with me* label was removed. The best part was, I didn't need to take medication. The irony you find in being an empath is that, we are supposed to feel. We are supposed to use our empath abilities to bring about greater compassion and connection. At the same time, it is important we protect our energy field. Think of it like a yin and yang concept—what you take on—you need to get rid of.

As you start to understand being an empath, the next question that comes is why? Why am I an empath? There are three truths I came to. The first truth is, you had trauma, and the trauma is what heightened your empathic abilities. Yes, most empaths are extreme trauma survivors. That trauma and what it did to your spirit, is what cracked it open. The second truth is that some souls are newer to the Earth plane and haven't been stuck in the human plane of social programming and low-frequency battles for centuries, so their higher vibration automatically puts them in the empath category. The third truth involves an individual that would have been raised in a situation where they were encouraged with their imagination, and creative thinking would also have been guided that it was natural to be this way. As a result the gifts were actively cultivated with the person as a child.

For about two weeks, I sat in a puddle of emotions at this realization and looking back at my life and all the times it had impacted me exponentially. My childhood made more sense. My romantic relationships had more clarity, and my interactions with the people I work or just interact with made more sense. It was at this part there was an acceptance of this as an okay thing. I am an empath. I just needed to learn how to go from being an unstructured empath to a centered and grounded one. Figuring out how to get your consciousness (spirit) and your mind in alignment to center yourself energetically, then to understand how you use your empath abilities in a safe manner and more easily. For how to manage your empath abilities more constructively, refer to the Healing Chapters. To read more on empaths, I suggest looking into Dr. Judith Orloff's books.

After two weeks of sitting in this revelation, I reviewed my notes from that psychic again. I had wondered what empath meant, and it stumbled me down this path. The notes said I was an empath and intuitive. That intuitive word. Did it also mean something slightly different than I thought it meant?

CHAPTER 5

WHAT IS AN INTUITIVE?

What did Da Vinci, Tesla, Rumi, Plato, and Einstein all have in common? They were all initiatives that leaned into their abilities. An intuitive, quite simply, is someone with psychic or extrasensory perception (ESP) abilities.

Here's Tesla describing a cell phone in 1926: "When wireless is perfectly applied the whole Earth will be converted into a huge brain, which in fact it is, all things being particles of a real and rhythmic whole. We shall be able to communicate with one another instantly, irrespective of distance. Not only this, but through television and telephony we shall see and hear one another as though we were face to face, despite intervening distances of thousands of miles, and the instruments through which we shall be able to do all of this will fit in our vest pocket."

Intuitive is an intuitive person is someone who senses something the average person doesn't. They use what is otherwise known as the sixth sense. Easy example: ever walk into a room, and you immediately get a very strong vibe against someone, and you don't know why? But you can't escape the feeling and what it is telling you to do, which is to get away from that person. That would be using your intuition. There are no facts in front of you that indicate anything is other than what it seems, but something else is telling you something is, in fact, off, something you just can't see, hear, touch, taste, or smell with the primary senses of your physical body.

Intuition is the basic construct of tuning into the feelings of your body and then interpreting the signals it conveys to your brain. Sometimes it is knowing what to do without understanding why or even how you do it. At its core, everyone has intuition—it is just some lean into it and others don't. The ones that lean more into their intuition improve their intuitive abilities. You know why women's intuition is so good and why it is called that? Because for thousands of years, women have been oppressed and suppressed, and we had to learn how to communicate with each other without speaking a word.

The term psychic is frequently used to cover any and all extrasensory perception abilities, channeling spirits, etc. However, the newer connotation is called intuitive and reads more like this: someone who has empathic, intuitive/ extrasensory perception abilities who intentionally uses them in some manner to determine something other than the primary senses.

As you learn more about ESP abilities, you will see that it is not a one size fits all topic, and there are capabilities beyond what you knew were even possible. Additionally, just because you don't have a broad spectrum of abilities does not indicate that you are not an intuitive.

Let's discuss the various areas of ESP and see if you identify any within yourself. The Clair's—clairvoyance, claircognizance, clairsentience, clairaudient. Clair means "clear" so clear sight, clear knowing, clear feeling, clear hearing.

TYPES OF PSYCHIC ABILITIES

Clairvoyance can actually take multiple forms. It is the one that most of the "psychic how do you know that shit" comes from. Different people "see" different things through their own filters, and it is important to understand that we don't all have the same gifts, and we don't all use the ones we have. Some people see spirits, others see energy in colors, and others can see other places or people. What is it that you can see that is not like everyone else you know?

For someone like Tyler Henry (Celebrity Medium), his clairvoyance is in symbols that his spirit guides use to communicate with him along with seeing spirits. He sees numbers and groupings, and he has built up his own library with his guides which is his language, and he knows how to interpret it. He sees and hears his spirit guides, and he sees and feels other spirits in his presence. For me, my guides simply won't participate with me in symbols. That isn't what they want me to do or learn and probably would be more of a distraction to me on my life path than of assistance.

My clairvoyance however, popped out at eighteen while doing LSD, and I can tell you, I thought I was going crazy because it didn't stop when the drug wore off. For my clairvoyance, I saw these little film-like clips of people clear as day. I would look at someone and then automatically, in my mind, see like a three second flash of someone's life at some point. All of the flashes were of really, nothing of significance. Might be a woman about forty-five who I see as a little girl, running down the front steps of her house. Might be a man who looked barely younger than now, and I see him checking out at a grocery store. It took seeing the images of the people who were closer in age to realize that at some level, this was not made-up in my head. But I still didn't know what it was and just thought I was losing my mind because this was happening 100 times a day. I literally thought, damn it, I did NOT SAY NO TO DRUGS and just LOOK at what fucking happened! I fucked myself up! As a kid of the 80s with the Just Say No To Drugs campaign everywhere, some of you will understand the depth of that and have a good laugh.

But because I didn't understand what was happening to me and because it happened in direct correlation with doing a drug, I literally did think I was losing my mind, so I mentally worked to stamp it out. I stopped looking at people and started looking down or around. It took about a full year for it to eventually stop. The point I am in today, however, in looking back and realizing that was simply clairvoyance capabilities occurring, and oh no, I could have been working to enhance them this whole time, and instead, all I did was suppress them. It does not make me want to do LSD again however. It just will have to be unlocked in a different way.

It took reading about people having different types of clairvoyance to understand that it had different flavors as well. Whether your sight is color based as in you can see energy in color around people and things as your clairvoyance and then what the interpretation of that energy field means. You could see spirits as your clairvoyance. You could see images like I did as if I was connecting into someone else's mind into a memory stored there. You could see symbols that you then identify to translate messages. Or maybe you can remote view, and your clairvoyance allows you to see into a certain place or event. I can also see random people in my mind that I have no idea who they are or where they are located. But they are very real and on this planet.

While my clairvoyance as it was when I was eighteen is not in play in that manner currently, I do have times where I have these same type of visions except not when I am looking at someone, and it is almost like I am telepathically transported to seeing out of the eyes of someone else. I all of a sudden see someone, and then they see me. Or whoever I am seeing through. I can see them clear as day, but I don't know who they are, or what their purpose is or why I am seeing "them." But I can feel as if I am there, wherever there happens to be in the moment I am tuning in to someone somewhere else on the planet. Other notable clairvoyants are Nostradamus, Edgar Cayce, Barbra Vanga, Da Vinci, Plato, Tesla are just a few. There are some modern-day psychics as well. Just search for prediction prophecies. I personally like Jeanne Mayell if you are looking for world prediction events.

Claircognizance is one of my favorites because I happen to have been using it for a long time intentionally but to some degree unaware. The best example of claircognizance would be to reference the film *The Matrix*. I don't know what you all thought after watching *The Matrix* for the first time, but I can tell you what I thought. The graphics were amazing, and the plot and everything else was mind-blowingly Hollywood cool, but I came out of that movie a little shaken like, wait, we should maybe talk about this whole plot concept here. I mean, did no one seriously have a moment where they thought, what if that shit is real, and we are watching a hologram of our real lives as batteries to alien assholes and are simply in a messed-up dream state. Like, seriously y'all, that was some messed up stuff that my brain just can't let go of.

In the first Matrix film after Neo was unplugged from *The Matrix,* and he is in the ship and they are explaining they have a construct like *The Matrix* where they are able to download training programs into one's mind like software. They pop in kung fu, and a few seconds later he is like … I know kung fu. Now, he was rusty in the practical application of it, and if you do not use it, then you will be too. He all of a sudden knew kung fu. Now, if they hadn't told him they were doing a download, then it would have been even more confusing to him on HOW he ACTUALLY KNEW that he all of a sudden KNEW kung fu.

For me, one of my lessons that was a light bulb moment was going back and looking at the things I just knew and consequently leaned into my knowing regardless of what anyone thought. Like my own personal secret. With my mother, I honed my claircognizance as a child. There were so many unspoken moments. Moments where I knew she couldn't or wouldn't speak her mind, but I knew what she was thinking. I couldn't explain how I knew, just that the thoughts and feelings I was experiencing when looking at her were as authentic as if they were my own thoughts and feelings. While it is cool to have, where it really bites me in the ass and is something I have been working to improve upon, is that because I "know," I start verbally overriding people. I know Kung Fu. My big trigger in using this gift in conversation is this.

Ever had moments in conversations where someone else is talking, and they are starting to stumble over their words on the idea they are trying to get across to you and then, BAM, you just know exactly what they are trying to get across and then also all of the thousands of interconnecting pieces that map out from there instantly, and you are like, yeah I totally know what you mean but in every direction that topic could go. For me, because I already know Kung Fu, my mind is ready to move on like a mile down the road. As a result, I come across as rude, even curt, and then cut the person off. Not exactly the best qualities to imbue, eh?

But the great thing is, now I understand. I understand that I have claircognizance and the ability to understand at an entirely different level, and that yes, I need to use that, but what I really need to do is, understand that the other person did not mentally go where I went. And while they were walking down a road thirty feet, I became the Flash and zipped all over the city and got the layout in five seconds. I can't explain how I know. I can only explain it feels like Neo when he learns kung fu in a moment.

Something that otherwise takes years of dedication to the craft and skill, now instantly, download complete.

The irony is, in many ways, this makes total sense to me. It's the same way I know stuff in my work environment before it happens, or how I can do the planning at work in minutes that normally should take at least a day mapping it out. Because my mind acts like a supercomputer in these instances that I have constantly honed over the years. It also, in some ways, is enlightening because instead of the … oh I just need to work on my manners because I am a Type A person, it's, no I got something different going on here, and I need to be the one to take an internal breath. Simply bask in the knowledge of knowing what I know, and then let the person complete their thoughts anyway. After all, I am learning, I do have the benefit of time, and not everyone has the same abilities.

Let me be clear, having claircognizance is not saying, you know everything, or can tap into everything. If you started having a conversation on a topic that I really have no basis of, say complex math, then no, my claircognizance will not take effect at all. For me, it is more triggered in certain events where, like okay, I need to access that now. I don't walk around my day where I know how everything will unfold or understand all the secrets of the universe as it only engages when I want to focus on something and solve something. Is my kid lying to me? I zone in, scan, employ telepathy and empathic intuition to determine if that is the case.

Along with many years of repetitive processes and systems, I have been able to predict how things will go down at work. I know the players. I have the luxury of past info to aid me, and guess who is right in the end? Yep, I am. My accuracy is pretty clutch when I engage it in any area of my job function.

Most of this is simply data points. Data points that get stored in my brain like a computer program. I have a library of strengths and weaknesses for all players in my data store, and a collection of data points that allows me to know how they operate as human beings, and as a result, my mind can compile how they most likely will respond to a future event. I understand where I can push and where I need to be accommodating or sensitive. So when data points come in on something that I have any level of data storage on or something that can liken to a data storage in my mind, then when I get triggered by "you know what I mean?" Yes, yes, I do in all its complexity faster than I could even speak it.

Dating for me is super hard. I just know immediately if it is a yes or no, and it is usually a no. The amount of data that descends on my brain about the individual in many ways is no different than what every single person does when they interact with someone. But for me, I literally can easily map out what the next twelve months look like including everything. I can see the end game really before it even begins. And thus I am like, well what is the point? Why do I want to waste time and energy on someone when I know it isn't going anywhere? Especially since I already know, I will be the asshole ending it. It's like if you came away with a lunch date with ten main themes or impressions. I walk away from that same inter-action, and now have the ten main themes: the map, the route each one goes, an assessment of feeling against that route is done in a flash, data is returned, and so … why waste my time doing this? I mean, I walked away with about 10,000 data points, and they all concluded this isn't "the one" so why bother because all I will really do is cause someone else emotional pain, and I will have been inauthentic with what I already knew to begin with. When someone says, well, you never know, you might be surprised. Actually, no. My consciousness knows.

Clairaudient is the gift of hearing. This one will start to open up most of your minds hopefully, if you start paying attention to yourself, stop discounting yourself, stop trying to trick your mind into believing some-thing different. This is where we "hear" our spirit guides, or just bodies of consciousness in general. Clairaudient is the one that first triggered me.

The voices—at least for me, come from my inner ear. Most of the time, it is a man. I don't hear him often but when I am driving or when I do something stupid, he says something. I didn't realize it until my Awakening that the voice was not mine. I mean, I had always heard that voice, but I passed it off as my inner voice. But, it was male, and my inner voice is not male. In other extreme situations I have heard other voices scream out at me as well. While some clairaudients are used to having spirits talking all around them, some only do when they tune in, and others barely hear any. I go over more of this stuff in the Spirits and Entities Chapter.

Clairsentient is where one can sense things about people or places that they shouldn't otherwise be able to. In some ways, it is a combination of other gifts as it relies on all your senses to pull this kind of information. One example would be to walk into a house and be able to feel the energy of three different families that have lived there and know a general feeling of what happened in that house. Clairsentience and empaths go hand in hand.

Mediumship or Channeling is where an intuitive will tune into a certain frequency to hear messages from entities they want to convey. This is a form of clairaudient.

Trance Channeling is where you allow a spirit to come inside you to deliver the message through you. I don't ever recommend anyone doing trance channeling unless you are an experienced medium first. Not all spiritual entities are positive ones. If you don't know what you are dealing with or how to determine the difference, then you should not do any trance channeling. Your body is your vessel to control, and it can be dangerous to allow other entities of any kind into it.

Precognition is where you know something is going to happen before it happens. It is a perceptive ability that is relative to either global events, events about those you know, or events that will happen. It can be as innocuous as doing something of no significance, to which when it happens, it feels like déjà vu. You can know someone is going to die. Or maybe some event will happen to someone near you, like getting pregnant, and you know before they are. It's basically having premonitions of the future. There are lots of people who have precognitive abilities that are rooted in near-term events. Having precognitive abilities like Nostradamus is more difficult. Additionally, far-reaching foretelling events have the ability to not occur because of the possibility of different timelines being put in play pending the free will choice options of major players involved in the Earth plane.

I have often had experiences where I have seen something for the first time and have gone, "this is not the first time I have seen this or heard about this." But how is that possible? Well, there are theories about parallel dimensions, that we have copies of ourselves living similar existences in different realms, much like they portray in the series *The Flash*. In fact, that is one of the theories about when you have a déjà vu moment. One of those parallel versions of yourself has already experienced that exact same moment, and it connects to you. Another theory is that there are moments you saw either in astral projection or lucid dreaming of future situations that you then experience in a conscious state.

Remote Viewing is the practice of seeking impressions about a distant or unseen target, purportedly using ESP and a series of process controls. Remote viewing is not restricted to current time, places, or events. The US military has been using remote-viewing techniques in their covert ops for decades. Ingo Swan, Russell Targ, and Pat Rice were the pioneers of remote viewing. Russia also had used and studied various psychic abilities for warfare uses. Various documentation on their work can be found online and in books. While remote viewing is a relatively structured technique as part of a way to deduce reliability, that doesn't necessarily mean it has to be. My clairvoyance currently allows me to tunnel in as a remote viewer through someone else's eyes, somewhere else on the planet. One thing to note, Ingo Swan did remote viewing of Mars going back a million years ago. From his accounts, it was colonized, but the planet was dying, and they were looking for another planet to live on. The account of some people going on a ship to a new planet sounds like Earth. Possibly even the Adam and Eve origin story.

Telepathy is the practice of transferring information mentally from one person to the next without using any of the five primary senses. Most people think of telepathy as being able to read someone's mind. But what if I explained telepathy in this way. Ever have an experience where you and another person were thinking the same thing at the same time, and one person verbalizes it to both of your surprise? Or you are thinking about a friend and all of a sudden the phone rings, and it is that friend calling? Telepathy is a form of energetic synchronicity. Have you ever been doing something of no significance, and out of nowhere you are thinking of a certain person you haven't thought of for a while and maybe it was a toxic relationship or maybe someone you miss, and you ask yourself, why am I thinking of so and so right now? Telepathy. The other person in that moment is creating a telepathic energy circuit back to you. For example, maybe you had an issue with a coworker, but it wasn't a positive interaction. Then you find yourself hours later randomly thinking of it, like a video feed that pops up in your mind and you are repeating the whole thing with the same intensity as before? Then getting angrier the more you think about it. Almost like you are escalating or intensifying the conversation more than the original conversation covered, meanwhile wondering, why am I SO intense and focused about this situation at this moment? Telepathy.

I like to rewrite it to be, telepathy is the mental projection of a specific thought or emotion toward a specific individual, intentional, and non-intentional, that implants in their consciousness. I didn't quite connect telepathy to what I was doing until writing this book. I had only seen it viewed straight from the energy plane as it relates to astral ties of people's aura field and hadn't tied that into the basic telepathy that many of us experience all the time. Before I discuss removing toxic energy from the people intermingled in your energy field, I want to explain the basis of it under telepathy first.

When two people are near each other in proximity, then their toroidal energy fields intertwine, even if they never touch. Communication and contact between those two people increase the energy connections made between those two people. The more two people intermingle their auras, the more connected they become no matter where they are in the world. In a relationship, you share all the chakras of your aura with that of your partner. So your chakras start lining up energetically. Then let's say the relationship ran its course, and it was a toxic one that ended badly, and you haven't seen them in a few years. Now you have that thought while doing the dishes. They pop into your head, and you are wondering why this popped up. Let's say it feels like a negative thought, and now, you are getting agitated remembering all the nonsense you put up with this person. You are even saying to myself—I dealt with this already. Why is this even coming back or coming up?

That would be because the other person is having an intense thought/memory of you. Through their mind, the energy connection engages, and the astral ties that you still share become active. Remember, energy has no boundaries through space and time. It just has to be given motion. A thought is a form of moving energy from one place to another. Now, if this connection is negative and it seems to build, well, they are having negative thoughts of you too.

It took me discovering this to understand why I was still having all this residual and compounding thoughts of my ex when I couldn't understand why. We were building upon each other. So one of us would be pissed about something, mentally project our feelings in our own space, then that transferred to the other person, who then would get angry, and project back to the first person, creating this awful loop of negativity. I decided I had to get that to stop. It wasn't healthy for either of us, and I was not mentally in that headspace and hadn't been for a while so it was confusing for me to understand why this was happening.

Before we go on to Telekinesis, I want to make one more comment. Ever been in a relationship and you are convinced the other person is cheating? You have no proof, but you know it in your bones. You may or may not know the full degree, but you know something is not right but you don't have any evidence that is tangible to the five primary senses.

Well, of course, it isn't right. If you have been in a sexual relationship with someone, and you have intertwined your energy fields consistently, then when another energy intermingles, you can feel the vibrational change between you and that person. You can feel a disturbance in the alignment of your chakras between the two of you. So yes, you were right. S/He WAS cheating! You KNEW it! Now what are you going to do with that knowledge? Are you going to continue to fight that knowledge, waiting for the evidence? Are you going to continue to sit in the ideology that they will change? Stop waiting for the proof you can see with your eyes, hear with your ears, smell with your nose and decide to respect yourself even if the other person doesn't respect you and get out of that relationship.

Telekinesis is the ability to manipulate objects or matter without actually touching them. The concept centers around tapping into the Chi (life) energy force and manipulating the vibrational frequency against that thing to make it move. While most of us are familiar with the spoon bending technique of telekinesis, I actually want to discuss the Chinese Super Psychics. Since 1982 the Chinese government has been identifying, studying, and supporting the work of psychics. To date, we know they have identified at least 100,000 children that fall under the criteria of a Super Psychic. We know they have been researching psychic abilities for military and medical research for decades. What has ultimately happened with the original batches of identified super psychic children is not real clear.

The Chinese are rich in belief of Eastern ideologies of Qigong energy practices, reincarnation, and higher levels of consciousness, so curating psychic abilities in children is not a stretch. There are children who can read messages folded up in a bottle. Levitate objects and a lot more things. There is a girl that can literally speed up the photosynthesis of a bouquet of flower buds and almost instantly make them bloom just by waving her hand over them. This is real. This is happening, and not just in China. But there is a distinct difference. China is encouraging the tapping into higher levels of consciousness and has been for centuries. Encouraging this growth in children, which is a good thing.

To suppress the abilities within a child is part of the overall problem. When creativity and imagination are stamped out due to the rigors of the real world, we stamp out the ability to connect into those dimensions. When we tell our children, you didn't see that, it didn't really happen, that wasn't real; what you really are doing is completely discounting their reality, and reinforcing back to the child that their mind is not to be trusted. Because they trust you, and you are telling them they are wrong, so they must be wrong.

Again after researching this information and concluding I had all the clairs to varying degrees and was an empath, I sat in a bit of bewilderment. I mean, I have gifts. I am a big purpose person. Everything has to have a purpose, even if it feels like a terrible purpose. As I sat in the knowledge and acceptance of having gifts but still something was nagging at me. Why do I have gifts? What is the purpose of me having these gifts? What does it mean? And what is this psychic stuff about really? Where does it come from?

It was at this time of discovery that I was first hit with the physical symptoms of an Awakening. To say that this was just a mental journey is far from the truth. I had physical changes that were happening to me so severe that when I did more research it led me right into thousands of other people awakening at the same time and going through the same physical experiences I was going through, wandering down the rabbit hole on this stuff too, which was pretty eerie. Why are we awakening and why now? That was a question that would haunt me in this process. There was something innately bigger in play here. I discuss the physical symptoms later on in greater detail.

In this journey, I was surprised to see certain names continuously popping up, but in a way, I had not previously been informed or led to believe. Well-known individuals who were/are intuitive in their day, and their work is riddled with discussions on consciousness, Da Vinci, Pythagoras, Carl Jung, Plato, Tesla, Einstein, Nostradamus, Barbra Vanga.

Carl Jung, in 1930, noted in a lecture the term synchronicity. His work has topics that were his astral projections and remote viewing capabilities and then discussions about the conscious mind and the interconnectivity of the mind. I honestly don't remember being taught this stuff in my college psychology class. Jung evening talks about how your path to enlightenment is essentially through the different energy centers of the chakras.

If you are interested in one of the most fascinating psychics whose channeling occurred in a state of trance, then I suggest looking into Edgar Cayce. Cayce endured his own conflicts between what he revealed in these trance sessions and his Christian faith.

Psychometry is the intuitive predicting of events associated with an object that belonged to someone. Have you ever picked up a ring, or a watch or an object, and it brought forth something to you? An image? A memory? That is psychometry.

Lucid Dreaming is a way to manipulate your dreams from a some-what conscious state. You know when you are in that place early in the morning where you aren't awake, but you aren't asleep, and you are coming out of something? But the dream feels very real in the moment? And you can sometimes tweak it to how you want it to be? That's kind of like lucid dreaming. However, you usually are in a REM sleep state when lucid dreaming.

Astral Projection is an out-of-body experience. Up to this point, I have used soul/spirit/consciousness to surmise a single concept. In this moment, we are going to add a fourth noun ... the astral body. Your astral body is your consciousness ... your soul ... your spirit. Basically astral projection is where you temporarily pop your astral body out of your physical body. At that point, you can see things clearer and in new perspectives because the human body density isn't mind restrictions are no longer in play. You can envision and see futuristic scenarios, past scenarios, etc. most people say you feel this intense buzzing right before you pop out. I've never done it, but I know quite a few that have. They seem to like it! The best example of astral projection is in the movie *Dr. Strange*.

CHAPTER 6

CONSCIOUSNESS AND SPIRITUALITY

Spirituality and science are not mutually exclusive but instead are connected. As we grow from children to adults, we are taught to limit, repress, suppress, and deny many things within each of us to conform to what system of control (social programming) we are raised within. What defines one's consciousness? By definition, consciousness is the state or quality of sentience or awareness of internal or external existence. In psychology, consciousness is one of the three primary states of cognizance. The other two being subconscious and unconscious.

In a true spiritual journey, you will find the discussion of consciousness dispersed throughout. Consciousness is essentially your essence of life, encapsulated in a collection of light-based energy that contains information in the electrical cells. Your consciousness is your soul, your spirit, your aura, your astral body. It is the part of you that has been alive for eons as you have inhabited denser three-dimensional vessels to have tangible experiences. It is the part of you that was created from Source energy and the part of you that will continue after your human body no longer can.

In this path, you find a few schools of thought. The first is that all souls were originally created from Source. Some people may want to transition that to being God, but it is not a God, so to speak, and not a God as defined in religions. Source simply exists. Source is light-based energy which means all conscious souls originated as light-based spirits or entities from the same place. Where that gets confusing is when you are up against an operator in this world that does not feel light based on the sense of peace, love, and light. The predominant spiritual theory is that all spirits came from the light, but over time, they have either raised in vibrational frequency, or they have descended in vibrational frequency. It can be difficult at first buying into this, but we all came from Source. That is why you feel a connection to something larger, but you can't quite put your finger on what.

The second theory is that new souls are always being created from Source. A third theory is that there are souls that came from a Dark Source. Whether you buy into the light Source only but within it, there was a split. Or the light Source is a split off from the dark Source, but they are still connected, it doesn't really matter. Within duality, you ultimately arrive at polarity.

Where things go sideways is this. Religion polluted our spirituality and our connection with Source. Your spirituality is what you instinctively know, religion is simply the rules that bind and enslave your mind. Your spirituality according to religions is primarily dependent upon the geography you are born into/raised in. But spirituality is separate from religion because religion is a man-made system. Not anything cosmically

Divine. They have taught you that you are not worthy and are separate from your Creator when nothing could be further from the truth. The only person or entity that will save you is yourself.

In every awful moment of my life and all the moments after, there wasn't anything else there making magic happen. It was me, my own mind, my own will, my own two feet, putting one in front of each other and slowly walking away from something that I needed to. No matter how bad the pain. But there was no God or Jesus carrying me through it. It was me and me alone.

Source isn't a God you pray to help you on your path. That isn't how it works. Source is a connection point. It is where we feel our greatest connection to all things, where we feel love and whole. What you will ultimately get to in this path is, humans were never meant to bow down or worship anyone or anything. That we are effectively our own creator Gods and were designed as such as part of an extension experience of Source. But then, we got cut off. We were told by priests we were not worthy, that we are sinners, that we must submit, obey like a dog, and hope we can make it to this mythical place called heaven. We sit in the frequency centers of shame and fear when we were meant to vibrate in the higher frequencies of love and joy. Our path to enlightenment centers around rising from those low frequencies to vibrate in higher levels.

In discussions on consciousness in the New Age community, they refer to it as dimensions of consciousness. 3D, 4D, 5D, etc. 3D is the current framework we are operating in. 4D is the next level of framework, and 5D is where you are able to be like Buddha in most situations. Simply recognizing situations for what they are and being able to move through them due to a certain level of understanding and compassion of the other people involved.

Note that dimensions of consciousness are different than actual different dimensions of space and time—which is often conflated in the New

Age talk. In some instances, you will see where 3D is the current dimension we are operating in. 4D is a dimension where negative spirits control the 4th dimension, and 5D is the dimension where we finally start to elevate ourselves in consciousness and are in a different dimension with high-frequency beings. The truth is, it doesn't really matter if you believe it is an actual dimensional plane or if it is simply a brain wave and frequency resonance. What matters is that you are working to improve yourself in the area of love, compassion, empathy, centeredness, yet maintaining appropriate boundaries with others, so they don't bring your vibrational energy down.

We are all connected. Only our beliefs, egos, and fears separate us. Human beings can only see 1% of the visible light spectrum. That means 99% of our existence is unseen. Let that sink in for a bit. We aren't seeing even half the picture. When you start meditating, you start connecting to that Source energy. You start to learn to turn inward to seek answers vs thinking only your religious figurehead has them.

We have twelve strands of DNA in our bodies today, but ten are dormant. Science has classified these strands as "Junk DNA" because they lack amino acids. Why are they dormant, and what could we do mentally and telepathically if they were not? I bet a whole lot. Did we once have this DNA active somewhere in our evolution, and was human DNA genetically manipulated? We only have the ability to actively engage 10% of our conscious brain at best. What if we could access 50%? What would that entail? Let me be clear. It doesn't mean that we aren't using the whole 100% of our brain as we are using it via our unconscious and subconscious levels, but our conscious mind simply is not engaged at a high capacity. We act like robotic trash cans operating on autopilot. Tossing out the things it deems not relevant in the current moment. It is because of this, we have filters in our minds that we create, and as we walk through life, those filters are reinforced, which form our belief systems about ourselves and others.

For more information on discussing consciousness in the current age, I recommend looking into Eckhart Tolle and Abraham (Esther) Hicks' work. They cover situational awareness and deconstructing the myth that you are not worthy. If you need a pick me up during this process, I suggest Aaron Doughty on YouTube. He has videos on how to elevate your consciousness and your vibrational frequency.

Additionally, several people including Helena Blavatsky have discussed the consciousness of Earth and the evolution of both the Earth and humans into different "root races." According to her, Earth has its own consciousness and root races are the markings of human evolution in intelligence and spirituality that have occurred over many millions of years on Earth. That as the Earth itself goes through her changes, so do the humans that occupy it. Don't forget, humans are in synchronicity with the bio rhythms of Earth.

Here are the root races as defined by Blavatsky:

+ The first root race (Polarian)
+ The second root race (Hyperborean)
+ The third root race (Lemurian)
+ The fourth root race (Atlantean)
+ The fifth root race (Aryan)
+ The sixth root race (TBD)
+ The seventh root race (TBD)

The fifth root race is called the Aryan Root Race. Coincidental?

CHAPTER 7

REINCARNATION

Old soul. You've said it at least once or twice in your life about a young child or a baby. They have an old soul. Let's think about this. How do they have an old soul if we only get one life? They can't. Then how can spirits differ in degrees of intelligent advancement? As well as why are some humans smarter than others? How do you explain the inherent difference between one spirit to the next? How do you explain child prodigies? Shouldn't we all come in with the exact level of nothingness, knowledge, and information? How do you explain people such as Einstein or Da Vinci or Tesla? Isn't that the consensus among the majority in the world? Handed down as fact throughout the centuries from Judaism, Christianity and Islam? You only get one life (YOLO), so make the best of it! Or … do you? You say it like we don't reincarnate but agree with the concept of an old soul being a spirit with advanced knowledge or wisdom.

How can it be an advanced spirit with knowledge and wisdom if it only belongs to this body and we only live once?

Reincarnation is not a new concept. Depending on where you were born depends on how open to this concept you are. If you were raised in an Asian or indigenous culture, you most likely grew up being taught about reincarnation, and that being the cornerstone of your belief system. If you were born in the Middle East or the United States, for example, reincarnation stands in direct opposition to monotheistic religions of Islam, Christianity, and Judaism. You are socially programmed to believe you only have one life. While all religions have some form of afterlife construct built into them, not all agree with the concept of your consciousness living on and having repeated life cycles of experiences. A belief in rebirth was held by Greek historical figures, such as Pythagoras, Socrates, and Plato, along with the Ancient Egyptians.

Reincarnation is a cornerstone of Buddhism and Taoism in which we continually reincarnate until our spirit reaches a certain level of consciousness that essentially is enlightenment. The basic tenets of reincarnation are that we are here to learn lessons and experiences, and in having those experiences, we create karma. In the process toward enlightenment, the goal of these repeated lifetimes is to clear those karmic cycles and find a way to bring balance to your soul in the form of polarity by freeing yourself from the constructs of duality.

There was a moment when someone said to me, "well, you know that reincarnation has been proven to be real right? They just concluded a forty-year study on it." I gave them a side eye and thought, this was something I definitely needed to look into further.

As I looked up the study by Ian Stevenson and continued by Jim Tucker, psychologists at the University of Virginia, it was interesting how they used certain correlations on the human body as a way to identify a potential life repeater. If a man got cracked over the head and died in a previous life, maybe he is born with a deformity on his skull indicative of what could be a scar of that wound. In Stevenson's adult cases, 70% died violently or unexpectedly. Then there were the experiences remembered by the individual (mostly children) in this lifetime about the previous one, which was then corroborated by still living individuals with no current relation. He found that the average span of time in these cases between death and rebirth was approximately sixteen months. Buddhism has a much shorter timeline of about thirty to forty days. Some other groups have different indications of how long in between lives we spend. In my research, it became clear that the timeline is not, in fact, definitive.

Beyond his study, there are actually lots of children that remember previous life events. You can check out the documentary *The Ghost Inside My Child,* which documents children who remember a previous lifetime and even identified what that life was. In some cases, the people they used to be connected with were still alive and were able to corroborate facts that otherwise could not have been known.

In all the postings I have seen asking about children, the number of people responding about things their children (or grandchildren) have said (mine included) that had to be from a previous life is uncanny. Instances of children telling their parents that they aren't really their parents. Or they lived in another time, or had another family. Or their child is doing things and saying things that they otherwise would have no framework for in this lifetime to know or do. When you discuss the child element, you realize that we have repeatedly enforced within children a certain reality for them, discounting their own, so it matches ours. "That couldn't/didn't happen." Even the concept of children saying they have imaginary friends, what if it is them seeing spirits? The common discussion is that children are very open up to the age of somewhere between eight and ten. Then most start to shut down those open channels, while some retain their open awareness of other things of existence.

I looked back on my life and dissected the types of people that resonated with me, resulting in a shiver down my spine. For example, witches are a very strong pull for me, especially during the Dark Ages. There were others as well, but it had me realizing, there was always a theme in those characters throughout the ages. Think about a movie you watch, and there is one character you identify with more than others. It's like that. So who do you identify with throughout the ages?

When I thought about my son, he had exhibited some behaviors from time to time that didn't seem consistent with a one-time/new soul concept. The first time he looked through his eyes was like a soul that woke up in a new body trying to figure out who these people are and where he is and what is going on. Every person coming into contact with him after that also got the same response as he discerned how he felt about that person. Most of the time, not wanting them near.

Doing meditation poses in parks randomly when I had never meditated in front of him nor did it at all. Things he would say that had me wondering how he could know that. What was even more surprising is when I did have a conversation with him about reincarnation and past lives; he leaned right into that in a heartbeat, seemingly relieved that what he had been experiencing in his mind actually was not made up or crazy. He now tells me about dreams he has had about other planets and experiences. Research this with your children if you have any and see what they tell you. Or look back at the odd things they told you in a new light, and maybe you will see synchronicities appear.

What about when you meet someone new, and it feels like you have known them forever even though you just met them. You feel a real connection that you just can't place. That is someone you had a previous life experience with. That is why they are so familiar. Your energy signature identifies with them on an energetic consciousness level.

While I never grew up learning much about reincarnation because that was heresy talk, I also had heard stories before that made me think it was a possibility, but more along the lines of six special kids and the Dalai Lama were the only ones doing it. Leaning into reincarnation concepts, mixed in with numerology, and soul contracts and you have an inherently larger construct of how spirits are operating in the loop of Earth lives.

That idea that we are all doing it and have been for thousands, millions, maybe even a billion years was a large perception shift. When you lean into it, you start to see the synchronicities at play and how everything comes together to make logical sense for once. However, if you grew up in a monotheistic religious household and are leaning into this for the first time, you have questions. How does it work? The whole thing, you die, you go where, how do you come back, what do you come back as, do you have a say, why can't you remember anything if the point is about karma and lessons and experiences?

The reason why most of us can't remember our past lives and more are answered in other chapters. But if you lean into this concept, you will see how it brings it all together and why all of this is so critically important to understand. If you can't get behind it or at least explore it, but still can get behind that humans are the only advanced forms of life in oodles of universes and planets, and we aren't that old, then you are stuck in a mental paradigm you can't break free from. Ignorance is when you fail to explore other avenues of thought as possibilities.

For me, this realization was quite sobering. I mean, to some degree, it made it feel like this lifetime wasn't really all that special. The relationships formed seemed to now feel like just some of many. Knowing I have had other children in previous lives. Other mothers, fathers, siblings, and even lovers. Which, of course, then leads you into the curiosity aspect of who are all those other souls and where are they now? Knowing the significance they had on me in my previous lives and the depth I felt for them was the same as what I feel for the people in this current life. Significant people in this life in some ways felt less significant in the larger scheme of things and at the same time, more significant because I was able to start figuring out pretty quickly which people in my life I had done this merry go round with before. Then a sense of understanding the difference in feeling when someone is part of your repeated life circuses or if they are just a random soul wandering through. While in some ways leaning into reincarnation was freeing and relieving, in other ways, it brought upon a newfound sadness of sorts. An ambivalence at this entire process of life. The fear of death and dying, now gone. The fear/uncertainty of never seeing loved ones who have died or will die after you was just gone. I mean, if your soul goes on, what is there to fear about that? You have already physically died many times before, and most of your deaths were not of a peaceful nature at an old age.

If you want to go down the rabbit hole on reincarnation and past lives, my suggestion is twofold. To read about the afterlife in between your physical life incarnations and what happens, I suggest reading the book Journey of Souls by Michael Newton. He is a psychologist who did past life regression hypnotherapy on his subjects and compiled from their stories the reincarnation process in the spiritual realm. If you want to read about general past lives regression stories, I suggest first reading the books by Brian Weiss: *Same Soul, Many Bodies*, and then *Many Lives, Many Masters*. There are other books with case studies by other lesser-known authors you can dive into as well. Once you have made it through Newton and Weiss, if you are still interested, then I suggest digging into the books by Dolores Cannon. She details alien abductions, higher self-discussions, other planets, the call of souls to Earth, and more. For reincarnation, past lives, and case studies, I also suggest the books by Edgar Cayce, one of the earliest individuals who did his own channeling in trance about the afterlife.

One interesting correlation in dealing with past lives and night terrors in children is that they appear to stem from a traumatic death in a previous life. If you are curious about your own past lives, you can find a certified hypnotherapist who offers past life regression hypnosis, which is specifically designed to also be a therapeutic form of healing. If you have fears or phobias, for example, that you can't deduce where they come from in an event in this life, past life regression therapy is good to identify where it stems from in one or more previous lives and then how to reframe the issue, so it no longer is a problem. Your soul retains with it the traumatic events from previous lifetimes with you as part of the wheel of karma until you are able to let go of that fear.

PAST LIVES AND THEIR CURRENT ROLE

At this point, I felt like I had a lot of themes and big realizations that hit me pretty quick, mixed along with the energy research and healing stuff I was reading about that was intertwining into all of this stuff. There were some topics that had come together and some ideas that should have pieced together, but I wasn't really understanding this Awakening picture fully yet. I had started out building a puzzle, only to feel it morph into a 3D puzzle, to then feel as if the puzzle was a building weighing on top of me with all this information that was making sense and connecting. The fact that it was all connecting was a bit horrifying. This was a complete shift from how I had been viewing my life experience and the world around me my entire life.

So what is the relevance of our past lives to our current lives? A lot. There are lessons and experiences we wish to have and work through, and if we don't make the desired choices as part of our blueprint, then we will have to repeat them in a future life until we work out the desired result. The result being something we learn and grow from and are able to evolve past. Because of that, everything in your current life is tied to things from previous lifetimes and experiences with souls you have known.

There are a lot of really bad things that have happened to our soul during these repeated lifetimes on Earth. All you have to do is take a walk down history and see all the war, famine, and oppression to know that you have lived through most of it. As a result, there are things that repeat into our current lifetime as a way to try and clear something. Sometimes it isn't even your karma you are trying to clear or break; maybe you went into a family that needed someone stronger in their light-based vibrational resonance to help break those generational cycles they couldn't get out of.

There are things that show themselves in this lifetime as a reminder. For example, if you have an unnatural fear of something but you don't know why, it is something from a previous lifetime. If you are afraid of water, maybe you died by drowning. It is the fear that you need to let go of. To come to terms with your past, forgive yourself, and let it go. Look back at your life and identify the things that seem a little out of place that you never understood why. Now look back at the things that seem oddly too familiar or comfortable, but you don't know why. These are clues into your past lives. People you feel a deep connection to, but you aren't sure why you feel that way toward them but not others? Those are souls you have had experiences with previously, and your energy recognizes their energy. What you should be getting to at this point, is that your soul is very old. And this is most definitely not your first rodeo living a human experience. In fact, most of us (soul wise) didn't even originate on this planet.

You can actually find information about your past lives. The two ways to do so are through past life regression hypnotherapy or through the Akashic Records. I will explain Akashic Records in the next chapter. Past life regression hypnosis, however, is where you change the frequency of your brain waves that allow you to access your memories at a subconscious level. Your soul level. The memories aren't gone from your soul, simply restricted in your physical body via the conscious mind. Your consciousness acts like a security guard, only allowing certain pieces of information that seem relevant moment to moment to pass through. Everything else is punted to long-term storage. It's a protection mechanism built into the mind. Our conscious mind only brings forth about 10% of memories it feels is relevant to our current situation.

PAST LIVES TRAP

Don't allow yourself to despair of things you may have done in your past lives. As humans, we have repeatedly made mistakes and poor choices. Some because we were duty bound into a system we had no control over. Find a way to hold your inner self, forgive, and let go. If you get stuck in sadness and pain and can't find your way through it, then it will have done more damage than good. It is in the past—you can't change it—you must have compassion for yourself if you are to clear it. That energy is stuck and needs to move. Because if it doesn't, then it cycles through your chakras (energy centers) and ends up making you physically sick.

If you pursue past lives through hypnosis, make sure the individual doing the hypnosis is certified in hypnotherapy. There are always people looking to take advantage of people in any area, and you want to make sure you are dealing with someone who isn't just going to help you walk down memory lane, but someone who will help you navigate past pain and clear it out properly.

Another trap is, maybe you believed you were someone famous or important? When the reality might have been you simply were in close proximity to that person in that life, and thus, your conscious mind wants to interfere with that concept. Or maybe when reincarnating to Earth, you used an imprint of a famous person as part of the overlay of your experiences to draw from. Maybe you were designing a path of leadership in this life so famous leaders of the past were an option to draw from.

You didn't actually experience that life, but the overlay imprint makes it appear as if you did.

The truth is, most of us have had some really crummy lives on this Earth history. If we were lucky to have a decent life, it probably was only one or two. When you look at famous people and their deaths, a lot of them did not die peacefully in their sleep. Many had traumatic deaths— Marilyn Monroe, James Dean, JFK just to name a few in the last one hundred years. It is normal to want to feel important. Important in the now, important in the past. But most of the time, our lives are simple and yet fraught with challenges because our true purpose is to make the changes within ourselves first. Clear the things that need to be released, learn our own lessons, make positive and loving impacts on those close to and around us. While it may not seem like you are taking down the empire, you alone are doing positive work that has ripple effects beyond what you can see. This is the most important work you could possibly do is to just be your authentic self. When one person does this, then another, and another, the ripple effects of that start to spread like wildfire. That is the ultimate goal. Instead of death by 1,000 paper cuts, it's more like conscious uplifting through a thousand kisses.

REINCARNATION TRAP

During this process, you have questions. How does it work? How soon do we reincarnate? If we reincarnate, how can people clairvoyantly communicate with spirits? If we are supposed to learn life lessons and clear previous issues, then why can't we remember what those issues are? I mean, wouldn't that be most helpful in the evolution of spiritual growth, if we could remember where we went sideways previously?

Why we don't remember is a very important topic. Some people mention that not remembering makes it a harder challenge, but in my findings, I am in conflict with that theory. I believe we are supposed to simply incarnate vs reincarnate. Doesn't it seem odd that we have karmic lessons to clear, but when we come here, all previous memories are wiped, and our blueprint is also a mystery? Any lessons to clear and look to remediate in a new human vessel should allow you to bring some of your memories with you even if it is just isolated to memories incurred during incarnations to Earth. We have experiences in order to grow, we have to learn our lessons, yet we create new karma and sometimes don't clear old karma and don't even remember what the old karma is. This perplexed me.

I felt like there had to be another trap when you die. There couldn't just be all these traps on Earth and not a final one when you actually die. This part is going to seem a little odd at first, but when you read the other chapters and come back to this, it will not seem so far-fetched. I stumbled upon it first when I was watching the video of the last interview with Max Spiers before he died. I didn't know who Max Spiers really was at the time and even had to look up who this guy was. He was a young conspiracy theorist who died under extremely suspicious circumstances.

What I found most odd as I was watching the video and what I would continue to find intriguing with most of the conspiracy theory videos and documentaries I watched is that almost all of these people were quite rational—even their speech. No one was acting like an out-of-control Alex Jones. Quite the opposite really. This had me realize, these aren't people who have lost their marbles. It was in that specific video that popped up randomly on the sidebar as I was looking for something else, where Max Spiers laid down the reincarnation trap. When I read *Journey of Souls* and had red flags popping up left and right as Newton outlined the trap, I knew this was the overarching trap in the reincarnation process of life on Earth.

"I don't want to go back to Earth. I like it here." Or "I don't want to go back, but I know I must."

If we have free will, as you will constantly hear repeated in this esoteric journey, then what part of NO I am not going back is not understood? Isn't that part of free will? The option to say no to something? Otherwise, if you are forced to go back and not allowed to go where you want to go, that certainly does not constitute free will. This was the crux for me. Free will as a human and free will as a spirit means you get the option to choose your path forward. You have the option to say, "I am done with this experience." Really though, if you have had repeated lifetimes of oppression, violence, starvation, poverty, among other things, why would you want to come back?

One theory is the possibility that an alien race created a False Ascension Matrix around our planet. In order to ensnare souls and send them back in, they created the Tunnel of Light. There is some dispute over whether the tunnel has projections of voices of the people you cared for that lures you into the tunnel or if actual spirits/guides are there to assist in getting you into it. But once in the tunnel, you go before a council that does a life review with you and tsk-tsks you on your life choices. You spend some time with your soul group and feeling happy and free of the human density experience. Then a new blueprint is drafted (one you actually create), then you go through a new tunnel that wipes your previous lifetime memories (mostly), and then they shoot you down into a family that you chose as part of your new blueprint. And round and round we go in this heroes and villains play. This school of learning. This holographic matrix. This game we are essentially playing, according to some. All of those are possibilities as to the greater picture we are simply part of.

Some people say that the moon contains the technology behind this False Matrix. Some indigenous tribes have stories going back telling of a time before the moon was there. For more on this moon idea—also see the Conspiracy Theories Chapter. The key to exiting the tunnel trap is first to know where you want to go before you die. You need to do a mantra on where you want your consciousness to go. If you encounter the tunnel of light, go anywhere but there. Your free will starts and stops when you choose to go into the tunnel. Maybe you want to go back to another planet. Maybe you want to go back to a starship. Maybe you want to stay in whatever density your consciousness ascends to. But if you get seduced by the voices or energy beings you see and the beam me up light, you will get sucked right back in. A decent reference resource for this topic is and links to other topics is ascensionglossary.com.

This theory, however, leads itself right into other theories. The film *The Matrix,* for example. That our consciousness is actually elsewhere. *Avatar* even had similar neuro links, and avatars that simulated a different body and experience. The idea that we are in a holographic matrix for some other more intelligent species to do their will with. Maybe they feed off us. Maybe it is a control mechanism. The idea of this life is a video game where we effectively get to play out all these scenarios, and really, there is very little harm because it is just a game. Dolores Cannon called Earth a school. A school for learning lessons. Albeit a hard school. You can decide for yourself after exploring these different pathways what you are inclined to believe.

What I do know is that after reading Newton's and Cannon's books where the question of what happens to the souls that do great physical harm to others and the vague answers that were given and lack of clear, concise answers provided by souls or their guides in channeling, is that there were serious gaps in the bigger picture here. The souls got extremely agitated at answering the question and did not want to elaborate.

To confound this idea is the notion that of all the regression case studies I have read to date of people with past lives, there are a few that mention serious harm to another individual in a previous life (as a soldier), otherwise, nothing on a large scale and no one in the current lifetime has committed these kinds of atrocities.

I would like to see a regression where serial killers or rapists are put under, and we get the details of their blueprints and hear what their souls have to convey. Was that part of their blueprint? Did they go off script? Because the idea that millions of us agree to be raped, murdered, beaten, enslaved, and it is just "part of the experience" or "karmic retribution" or we are "just actors in a great play" and we need to sit in the zero space of it isn't a big deal, or we just need to forgive and rise above, seems and feels like horse shit by people who have never experienced that kind of horror and all the nuances of it in the human experience. So much so that it is an avenue I plan on going down to find out the answers in the coming years.

CHAPTER 8

NUMEROLOGY, BLUEPRINTS, AND SOUL CONTRACTS

Numerology has ties into astrology, alchemy, and zodiac calculations. When you are born, where and to whom is all intertwined in your blueprint you designed for each lifetime. Before I get into numerology, blueprints, and soul contracts, I want to illustrate the synchronicities of numbers found throughout the ages. Clearly there is something behind numbers.

THE NUMBER 7

✦ 7 days of creation in the Bible
✦ 7 days of the week

- 7 Wonders of the World
- Book of Revelation, 7 churches, 7 seals, 7 trumpets, 7 stars
- Koran has 7 heavens
- In Mecca, Muslim pilgrims walk around the Kaaba 7 times
- Hindu there is 7 higher worlds and 7 underworlds
- Hindu weddings the bride and groom walk around the holy fire 7 times
- Baby Buddha rises and takes 7 steps
- 7 Planets in old astrology
- 7—our memory capacity, according to George Miller, is that people retain 7 pieces of information in their short-term memory. That is why phone numbers were 7 digits.
- 7 colors of the rainbow
- 7 notes on the diatonic scale
- 7 elements of music
- 7 numbers in the Roman numeral system
- 7 Dwarfs in Snow White
- 7 lucky Gods in Japan
- 7 stars in the Big Dipper
- 7 continents
- 7 oceans
- Tangram—7 flat shapes in a square
- Opposite sides of a die always equal 7 when added
- 7 rare gases
- 7 alchemy metals
- 7 orifices in the human head
- 7 bones of the tarsus in the human skeleton

THE NUMBER 12

+ 12 Rays
+ 12 Disciples
+ 12 Tribes of Israel
+ 12 Zodiac Signs
+ 12 Months
+ 12 Greek Gods
+ 12 Chakras
+ 12 Thoracic Vertebrae with 7 Cervical and 5 Lumbar
+ 12 dimensions to enlightenment

The basics of converting numbers to a mathematical calculation was founded by the famous mathematician and scholar Pythagoras. He started his theory of numbers by discovering a numerical relationship between numbers and musical components. He found that the vibrations in stringed instruments could be mathematically translated. From there, he looked at applying the same kind of mathematical concepts to other things. In doing so, he came up with the Pythagorean Method, where each letter of the alphabet corresponds with a number one to nine.

There are actually three schools of numerology thought, Chaldean, Kabbalah, Pythagorean. For our purposes, we are sticking with Pythagorean. Note that while the Pythagorean method is used in current numerology, Pythagoras himself did not use it in conjunction with soul-life concepts. Numerology, in many ways, acts like astrology with predictive interpretations about a person's character and purpose in this lifetime.

The Pythagorean method in numerology uses an individual's legal name and date of birth. Numerology assumes that you chose your name before you are born, subconsciously implanted it with your parents to be, and that is how you get named. You could say, no way, I hate my name.

Perhaps! But that wasn't the point of the name you chose. It had to work in conjunction with the family you would be placed with. Even in astrology, there's a concept that you chose the timing of your birth to correlate to certain well-established Zodiac indicators.

1. Each letter is assigned to a number 1 to 9.
2. From there, it is a series of adding and reducing to come up with a final number reduced between one to nine to determine your life path, soul urge, expression and destiny.
3. Life paths are correlated to each number as a mission that serves as the main theme the individual marches toward or has chosen to experience during their life.
4. Then, there is a blueprint that ties directly into it and comprises the overall experiences to learn/endure/resolve in this lifetime.

There are a lot more details you can find online about numerology information and life paths and translations to see how your name and number match up. There is your soul urge or destiny, life path, and personality number.

+ Expression # correlates to talents, abilities, and shortcomings for this life
+ Personality # correlates to your personality
+ Soul Urge # is the things that you yearn for or motivates you
+ Life Path # is the type of person you want to be in this life

For a specific reference, I suggest watching the videos of Gail Minogue on YouTube. She has a great way of explaining how numerology and blueprints work.

BLUEPRINTS

If the life path is the mission statement for this lifetime, then the blueprint is the main series of experiences you want to accomplish here in order to hopefully break past karmic life cycles either in your line or in a current family line in the quest to reach individual enlightenment. Think of it like a series of boxes that you need to experience or agree to experience. Your spirit guide(s) are aware of your blueprint, and part of their job is to ensure that maneuvers are put in place for those experiences to occur during your life.

Understand that many of these experiences aren't the wonderful everything-is-awesome experiences. They are designed to stretch you, test you, see if you can get past the challenge. Your blueprint is designed by *you*. Don't like your life? Then you either aren't following your blueprint, and your guides are intentionally trying to maneuver things to get you to make a different decision, or your current desire isn't in your blueprint. Or, maybe it is in your blueprint, but part of your blueprint is designed as a test you need to work through and pass.

It was at this point that the big question that started me running down these rabbit holes all of a sudden clicked, and I finally had my answer. The reason why the universal law of attraction and manifestation completely failed for me.

In this process, I did a lot of reverse engineering on well, myself. I knew who I was very well before my Awakening. I mean, I am that friend you want on the desert island stranded cause besides the laughs we will have, I will be absolutely committed to whatever course of action we feel in our best interests for survival and getting off the island back to the mainland. So if my higher self knew who I was at my core, and I had designed this experience, what did I get to? Well, the spirituality stuff, I would have been like, yeah, I get it, I should probably meditate a little more, have a nice day. The reincarnation and the deception of the human race, same, would have been like, interested to discuss so I can maybe learn something new, but you know, what do you expect me to do? The psychic stuff though, that cracked me, and everywhere it led me from that moment to the next piece of information that also validated against other information I was finding, and it was all making sense. Horrifically, but it was making sense.

I remember having this consistent vision. I was looking at two plain rooms with a shimmery watery barrier in between. There were two of me, one on either side of this shimmer. The version on the left had me looking a little bored and confused, like why am I in this room? Not even noticing the shimmery barrier, but instead, like in a police interrogation room where it was a reflective mirror, and I didn't realize there was another side. The right-sided me was looking at the left-sided me through the barrier, and occasionally yelling and just being a little frustrated that I couldn't see through this mirror. It took me a few weeks to work it out as I didn't quite understand at the time. But it was the veil. I was seeing myself from the side, where I was on both sides of the veil. One side oblivious (my human side) and the other side (my higher self) trying to have patience with the other. The veil is the barrier between the human plane and the astral/spirit plane.

In short, I wouldn't have fallen down this rabbit hole, unless I challenged universal law, and it failed me. It was the only way I would seek out a different avenue or answer than what was in front of me. I had to believe something to my core, engage universal law, and have it not work. Your blueprint can do that. So here I was again, back in the headspace of being pissed off at myself again. I did this to myself. I'm such a stubborn, determined individual, and I had to essentially outsmart myself. I mean, hats off to my higher self, but my 3D version on Earth was a bit pissed off, mind you.

I was annoyed, and it would grow as I went further in my journey, and I entered the land of love and light and consciousness, creating your own reality, manifesting your heart's desire, ensuring your work was more of service to others, and finding your soul's true purpose. Because at that point, I sat in the reality of, I just tried to manifest my heart's desire with every fiber of my being thank you very much and now I have nothing. It took me years to get to what I wanted to do. Sure it was lofty and grand, but the opportunity existed. The possibility existed. This would have been a grand push in the realm of the rise of the Divine Feminine on a global scale. Thus, I sat in an empty space for a few months on this "create your reality" speak littered among all this information. I was tired of being burned on new ideas and working on things that don't work in the moment, but ten years later it is viable, just for others. Tired of being a trailblazer. Tired of being in toxic career situations. Tired of not having a treasure trove of ideas of anything I wanted.

SOUL CONTRACTS

Back to the blueprint. In order to achieve these experiences, you make what is called soul contracts with various other light-based spirits. They have their blueprints, and it all intertwines. There are no coincidences about the people you meet that have a major impact on your lives. It was all planned to happen during this lifetime in some manner. The soul contract could be of any variety. Maybe it is to come in and be a catalyst for you, or maybe you for them or both of you for each other. Maybe you make a contract to go in as a mother and daughter situation. If you are a parent with more than one child, have you ever felt like you have an extra special connection with one of your children? Usually, the contract was made with you specifically, and often you had a previous relationship with that spirit. Sometimes spirits choose to go into the cycle but in a different way. Soul contracts can also be in a romantic way. You make contracts with spirits to come into your life and for you to learn from the situation and see if you make a different choice than you did before. Some are for the better, and some are for the worse.

Another aspect I had to work through was the idea that my intuition had directly led me into what I would consider bad relationships or bad experiences. As a result, how could I trust my intuition moving forward if it made me feel so sure about something and that something was not what I would consider desirable by the end of it? Well, that was still a contract I made. So the depth of the feelings is what was tied into the contract, and your intuition led you directly to it because your blueprint was designed to do so. Seems kind of like a poorly built plan, right? Well, without the bad, you can't appreciate the good. Without the pain, you can't rise above because you wouldn't even realize there is something that you need to rise above.

SOUL CONTRACTS TRAP

There is a lot written about Twin Flames, Divine Masculine, and Divine Feminine Soul Mate, Soul Mates.

Let me clear it up for you. It is just a soul contract.

Repeat that again. It is just a type of soul contract.

You made a few romantic soul contracts for this lifetime. The one you think is your forever soul mate right now might not be, or it might not even be your higher self's actual spiritual soul mate. Do you have someone you made a contract with to be a soul mate in this lifetime? Maybe, maybe not. This specific topic really spun me around as I looked at other people appearing desperate about this and arguing over what constituted a soul mate. It was almost as if they lost their minds on this aspect.

But at the same time, I also understood it. Understood it in a way that made me feel compassion for them. The root of happiness and joy is centered in love. End of story. Your most powerful chakra? Your heart chakra. Vibrational frequency resonance of love, right below joy. It is innately within us as human beings to want to seek out that euphoric feeling of love. We know what it is like, we know it is possible, but we become so desperate to get it that we sacrifice elements of ourselves in the hope that a certain person we are attracted to feels the same way. And if they don't, then we essentially try to force that person to fit the mold we want. Getting frustrated when they don't. When you read stories of life between life hypnotherapy, they all mention feeling lighter and somewhat euphoric when connected to Source directly. Sometimes I think we are searching for those who remind us of how we feel when connected to Source.

Do not get spun up on this whole divine feminine/masculine/twin flame nonsense. You have had a lot of romantic soul contracts over the course of this process on this planet. It can feel a little odd, sitting in the knowledge that you have loved a lot of people through the ages, maybe some of them several times over. But an important thing to understand is that love is fluid. True and pure love has no judgment or jealousy. It also has no gender constructs.

The second trap I want to mention is this. There is a running theme in past lives that we made contracts with ALL the people who were major players in our lives. If you are an adult, then yes, this is accurate. But if you were a child, then you may not have made a soul contract with a specific individual, and instead, you have a "by association" contract. For example, it may be that your parent made a contract with a soul, but you didn't. And maybe that contract was a romantic partnership of your mothers that brought with it sexual trauma or physical abuse at your expense. Because you sat in a space where she was in a contract with that person and made certain decisions, then by association, you were subjected to that individual. It does not necessarily mean that you chose to make a contract to sit in a place to be sexually or physically abused. I would wager that most people who disagree with this are humans that have not experienced abuse or trauma in this lifetime.

When we talk about clearing ancestral trauma, the idea is to break the cycles that have been repeating on the planet. To ensure you don't go from victim to perpetrator. This is a combination of changing your DNA via the concept of epigenetics as well as not inflicting trauma on another human. There is something inherently wrong with a batch of human souls, and to sit in the space of saying, oh, it is all just a game like there is no real harm and we are just learning, is a dangerous mindset. There is a bigger picture at play here. What we know is that we don't know the whole spiritual picture going on above us at higher levels of consciousness and other dimensions. I can tell you, if you believe there is no conflict in them, then you are mistaken. If you find yourself struggling with that, ask yourself, "Does your soul resonate with the idea of you wreaking great physical and or emotional harm on another human and thinking it really is no big deal?" I didn't think so. Something else is in play here. I don't have the answers, but maybe one day, my thoughts on this will be more fully baked and can provide clarity then.

With that said, there is another theory out there. If we take the concept that we are in a holographic matrix of sorts, then there are what are called non-player entities. Although they look and act like humans, they really are just a highly programmed AI to test and provoke your emotional energy. Think of Agent Smith of *The Matrix*. So the humans that commit the higher-level atrocities, are in fact a type of AI. Who are these? Well, if I had to take a guess, the easiest to identify would-be individuals who are psychopaths—people who lack proper emotional responses and commit horrific acts against others with no remorse. Whether this is the true reality we are operating in or not, I leave it to you to explore that possibility. I just know I can't entirely rule it out, so therefore, one more thing to go on the mental shelf.

CHAPTER 9

AKASHIC RECORDS

U p to this point, I was operating with a healthy dose of cognitive dissonance. I was teetering on the fence, one leg in my old mental framework, one leg hanging in the new mental framework. In looking back, Akashic Records was the point where my cognitive dissonance psychologically split me in half, rebuilt me on the other side of the fence and was the real push down the rabbit hole and me running the gauntlet at full speed. I had to know. I had to know it all.

My spiritual Awakening was not lengthy or wonderful. It literally felt like I was running a gauntlet of tests and information in a time trial. Each piece of information causing conflicts with what I had previously been led to believe, stacking on top of themselves unveiling a horror larger than I had imagined. When I hit Starseeds and reincarnation, things made more sense. Those two concepts led me very specifically to a couple places. I had started waking up to the idea I pretty much had amnesia. I had been mentally wandering around in a dirty swamp for decades, carrying a backpack of trash that served no purpose. I walked out of that swamp, threw the backpack down, got my bearings, and took off on the path ahead of me.

The impression my spiritual guides implanted with me was, "It's about time you wake up, you are behind, get up to speed because you don't have a lot of time. Write this all down because others need to see the bigger picture that many haven't been able to. They are stuck in one aspect and are not progressing."

It was rather eerie how every time I came up against something where I was confused, I was lead to another piece of information and how fast the answers appeared. I could have a thought and then within five minutes find exactly what I was looking for. If there was something that I knew I still needed more information or wasn't sure how it would connect, I just put it on a mental shelf, and then it would connect within a few weeks somehow. It felt like I had a pirate treasure map I was following that was not a direct line to the treasure—more like winding all over but on a specific path, so it would make greater sense in the end.

It's almost like you want to try to find things that won't validate, because then you can say you are making this stuff up. That it is all in your head. But when your information is getting validated, and it is resonating in a way that you can't dispute, it's both calming and unsettling because things make more sense than they ever did. Still, it is changing your entire core belief structure. You lean into synchronicities instead of dismissal with the term coincidences. For me, I felt like I was being both pushed and pulled into this process to keep pursuing things until I felt I had reached an end. There isn't anything further to discover except details that might fill in the gaps or add to what you already know. Leaving you wondering if you will ever get to the overall arching picture, which feels more like uncovering a web of deception. As the web grows larger and larger, it becomes more horrifying.

So what are the Akashic Records? Akashic Records are a compendium of all human events, thoughts, words, emotions, and intent ever to have occurred in past, present, or future lives that are encoded in the energy cells of our light-based spirits. In short, this is the Book of Life. The Book of Your Spirit's Life. Every single thing your spirit has ever experienced in this lifetime and all previous ones, no matter what physical body you inhabited or where is recorded in your Book of Life. The collective of all spirits Books of Life is stored in the Akashic Records which is the esoteric library. They are encoded in a nonphysical plane of existence (the 0 plane) known as the etheric layer. In today's age, you can think of the Akashic Records like we think of "The Cloud." Where data and information are stored in some other place that we can access remotely. Is it really that much of a stretch to envision that as a possibility seeing as the universe (and other universes) are billions of years old?

Your aura, which is an electromagnetic field of energy, or your personal ionosphere, transfers this information to your book of life in the ethereal plane. That is how it gets recorded. Your aura has a form of DNA encoding. Experienced psychics can access Akashic Records as a guide with you, unless you learn to do it for yourself, which you can. You simply have to work on intuitively tapping into this place on the etheric plane in a particular way. The rule to accessing records in the library are, you can only access your personal records and that of your child while they are still a minor child. Karmic rules don't allow for you to root around in other people's Book of Life without their expressed conscious permission. Your legal name and date of birth is energetically tied between your human vessel on Earth and into your Book of Life on the etheric plane as a legal contract. Your Book of Life is for you to access information that will help you move through your current life challenges. Doing so will expand your consciousness into a higher dimension of thinking and operating as a human being and a light-based soul.

After reading what Akashic Records was, and having already leaned into reincarnation by this point, the basic premise made sense to me. Akashic Records is a tool. Plain and simple. If you use the tool as intended like a car, then it is useful and serves its purpose. If you take advantage of it, then it can become an emotional weapon against you. The purpose of accessing your Book of Life is to resolve karmic cycles and understand how the past is relevant to your current life. You do that by evaluating your current life and seeing where things have gone wrong, chaotic, maybe they still are, emotional hang-ups like an irrational fear of something. Then you access the Book of Life and figure out what happened in a past life, and then review your current one again and see how that fits. Most likely, you will have a similar situation to a past life situation that had a specific ending. What happened in that situation? What was the bad stuff? Cause the bad things are the experiences that expand your mind as a human and your spirit as well. Have you in your current life resolved the same type of issue? Did you make a different choice? What did you learn from before? What do you still need to learn or resolve?

After stumbling upon this, I stepped back in shock and thought, wait a minute. Are you telling me that I can recover ANYTHING about myself even if I can't remember it? In a way that does not involve hypnosis? That there is a way to find out something you otherwise might not consciously know or remember or realize? I felt like I had found a golden egg.

For most of my life, there was something about me I couldn't explain. I had all the symptoms of a victim who had been sexually abused as a child, but I couldn't figure out why. I was extremely confident of the *who* did it to me, but I couldn't figure out the how and when and why I couldn't fully remember. I had sporadic images in my head as I became a teen. Eventually convincing myself I had imposed them on myself simply because I perceived something had happened by a certain person due to that hatred of said person for all the other types of abuse toward me, my mother, and my brother. I even remember as a teenager telling myself at points … you need to be very present mentally. Like, remember this because you feel like you aren't remembering a situation or situations somehow. As an adult, those images would take on a more horrific elaborate mind of their own. Something I would never tell anyone about.

It wasn't until my twenties, when reading about sexual abuse victims and the symptoms one has, did I realize I have or have had all these. Except, I had never been sexually abused that I could consciously remember. I had one incident when I was ten at a nondenominational church camp where a preacher tried to. I had gotten stuck being introduced to him by one of the ladies at camp after outdoor church service. He was a friend of my stepfather. We started chatting, well, he was chatting to me in a very even tone and trying to hold eye contact all the while talking about sin over and over and patting my leg, giving it a squeeze every few seconds. Slowly inching his hand up my leg until he got to my panties over a period of about ten mins. I remember at the time hearing this voice telling me, "Leave. I needed to get out of there NOW! I remember hearing my own inner voice saying, this doesn't feel right. Again the voice screaming at me to GET OUT OF THERE. LEAVE. LEAVE NOW!"

Once his finger moved over the lower part of my panties, I bolted up and said, "I have to leave now, bye." And I ran off. That was it. I didn't tell anyone. I had questioned whether I should tell my mother when I got home, but I decided that who would she believe? A man of God, a friend of my stepfathers, an adult, or a ten-year-old girl who sometimes tells white lies like, "No, I didn't sneak out of my bedroom to grab an orange after refusing to eat my dinner of liver and onions."

I had ended up repressing that memory until I was seventeen when it came flooding back to me after a conversation with a friend triggered it. That wasn't even that bad of an incident as it could have been, you know? That can't be it. So here I am going, how do I have the symptoms of sexual abuse, but there aren't any actual events, no real conscious memories? I have distorted images in my head of one specific person, but I couldn't place any specific event. Is it repressed? It must be. I was confident I would remember some sort of non-consensual physical encounter. I would have had defensive wounds for days that I would not have forgotten about. I would have fought to the death to stop it. Every time I tried to deduce when/how it happened, I kept drawing the same conclusion that it was in my sleep, and it ended with my conscious mind telling me I would have woken up.

When you become a parent, an interesting thing happens. You start going back down your own childhood in your mind. The good memories, the bad. Remembering where you were at a certain age and what you were thinking about or interested in. Even if you don't want to go back down that path, your mind takes you there over time. When my son hit the age of seven, I started having this cognitive dissonance show up again in the area of me being sexually activated early. I would ask my son questions every now and then, any cute girls/boys in class? I would get a "gross" look. I would scrutinize his behavior and realize his behavior was not reflecting my own childhood behavior. In a way, that was relieving for him, and horrifying for me.

I was masturbating as early as six. I was aggressive. I was into boys. I thought that was just who I was. I realized he wasn't having any weird anatomy discussions with his friends either. I had one friend who I look back on with sadness and go, oh good god, she was activated early too by someone. As the years ticked on and my son showed no further signs of this, my own internal panic grew. Something wasn't right … with me. I am not going into hypnosis to figure this out, and I cannot believe, for the life of me, I repressed something so heinous. For most of my life, the idea of doing hypnosis was a complete nonstarter. I no longer feel that way about hypnosis after doing more research on the subject and how it works.

Growing up, I always felt extremely uncomfortable around my stepfather, as did most people, a piece of information I gathered from a lot of people throughout the years. My mother's side and adoptive father's side of the family did not like him at all. When I was a month shy of three, my adoptive father died. A year and a half later, my mother went on a cruise and came back married. We moved a month later, halfway across the country to Missouri, and had instant family. It wasn't a situation where either parent looked at it like, we know this will be tough, and we understand there is a natural transition, and we will work through it. Nah, it was more like—this is the new law now, and get used to the new program. That new law was not loving, compassionate, or nurturing in any way.

The first Christmas, I was left crying after being told that those were traditions with my old father, and he was dead and not coming back. This is how we are doing things in this house and get over it. My childhood experience is a weird one all around. There are some bright spots for sure, but the traumas far outweighed the benefits. My stepfather was severely controlling, rude, demanding, demeaning, disrespectful, and just a really angry nasty man—one who also happened to be a very respected doctor in the area. From a psychological standpoint, he would be considered a narcissist and a psychopath.

I witnessed the emotional and mental abuse of my mother by him and would get so angry. As I became a teen, I became more enraged by it and more emboldened. My mother would always tell me to back down, and I would get so frustrated by her for not standing up for herself as a human being. I couldn't handle his complete disrespect of women. How he would cut her down verbally in front of friends, coworkers, family, anyone really.

The once graceful woman would calmly just go quiet. Watching her be silenced felt like it was killing me. I now know why.

I am an empath, so I was feeling my mother feeling her own silencing. Not to mention she is the one person I unknowingly practiced my telepathic abilities with since I was a child. I would stare at her at moments, like we could speak through our eyes to each other so it couldn't be heard. I would try to read her thoughts, so I would at least know her truth because I could feel it. The constant emotional and verbal abuse she went through, and knowing I only saw the half of it. We were a family of yellers. You yell when you are angry, accuse, stand staunchly in your being right on whatever the issue was, and then get mad enough to the point someone just walks away, goes to sleep, wakes up, and pretends it didn't happen. This was how my conflict negotiation skills were formed, and in which I had to learn to undo this terrible approach and learn a new approach in my adulthood. An approach more calmly handled and with a positive outcome. To complicate my mother's journey, she fell into a deep depression when I was about eight. My brother ran away. Stole the car, took a gun, and made it to Florida before being caught. Then he got sent to rehab for six months. My mother became fractured and began taking lots of prescription medications and became a hypochondriac about various illnesses. She ended up getting attention this way, and thus it became a repeating cycle for the rest of her life. It was also this time she and my aunt had a major fight and didn't talk for at least five years—the reason for the fight she would never divulge to my brother nor I.

I saw how he treated my brother. I saw how he treated other people. I would ask why he didn't have friends. He would say he didn't need friends. He would isolate my mother to where she lost all the friends she kept working to have when he came around. My own friends and even some of my brother's friends had told each of us to never leave them alone in a room with that man. Then there was how he treated me. I always got the impression he looked at me like I was just a mutt. An adopted kid, his wife picked up, and now he has to deal with me. There were the looks both inappropriate and the ones of disgust combined with the inappropriate things he would say as I went through puberty. The demand is that I have my school sports' physical done by him. And I mean a full-on physical examination you would do when you go to the gynecologist. Oh yes, he was an OB/GYN. After that, I told my mother that would never happen again. When I started my birth control pills and had to have routine exams, I went to another doctor in the clinic. He became irate when I said he was not going to examine me. After all, he had examined his own daughters, delivered their babies. What is so wrong with this? Umm, a lot.

When I was fourteen, he decided he didn't like my talk-back to my mother, which was really me trying to stand up for her and for myself, and he started physically assaulting me. He would chase me until he caught me, and then throw me to the ground. I would fight him until he got me in a position I couldn't get out of, then he would sit on my back and play patty cake with my butt. Know that he never spanked me as a child before this. Discipline had always been done by my mother.

When I asked her why she allowed this, she told me I was getting too big to discipline. I remember thinking, this is the point you ground me, not this weird assault shit. That went on until I was almost eighteen, and I finally left the house one night and told my mother the next day that I thought her husband was going to rape me. For years throughout my teens, every night I would go to sleep, I would crawl in my bed, bring the covers up to my chest, all the while looking at the door and thinking to myself, "I hope tonight is not the night he comes through that door and if he does, I hope I am physically prepared and strong enough to fight him off."

When I left for college, I told myself no matter what, I wasn't going to ever move back. Every time after that I had to go back to visit, I got anxious. I didn't really know why. I just got anxious. As I got further away from living there and then had to go back home to that situation occasionally once or twice a year, my behavior started getting worse. I would get massive rolling panic attacks for a solid week out leading up to it. I wouldn't know why but I would constantly shake and get volatile. I wouldn't sleep and felt like I was vibrating like an angry bull in a small, trapped space. My exes would ask me the same thing with the same wide concerned eyes, what is wrong? "I don't know," I would say to them while shaking and feeling confused. Why am I feeling this way? What is wrong with me? Why do I get like this? I mean, I know I hate going back because it reminds me of my childhood, but this seems extreme. What is going on with my body? I would cry at times. It was awful.

So when I was looking for another Akashic Record reading, a woman I had seen before offered them. I looked into it and decided this was the path I needed to take. I was tired of feeling like all roads led to the same town, but when you got there, there was no town. I discovered in Akashic Records, it was because the town had been cloaked. It was there the whole time, it had just been disguised.

Before the session, I had put together a list of things I wanted to find out. As I read over the list, I knew that some would not be answered simply due to time. I also knew that one was rising above the others as the most important. The one that felt a sense of I need to know NOW. The unknown/unconscious memories of abuse one was really weighing on me. We asked if I had any repressed or unknown memories of sexual abuse in this lifetime. I was not interested in any abuse my consciousness was already aware of, only things I wasn't aware of, if there was any.

She immediately started out at age five with lots of chaos in the house. I about fell over. That was when my life irretrievably changed from that point forward. She continued, "This is weird. You are unconscious or asleep." The rage of anger was now rising in me. I had come to this conclusion many times. Each time I discounted it because … I would wake up. The psychic then said, "This man is diabolical. He is evil." Then she said, "This is gross and feels … clinical." Clinical. She said the word clinical. Right after she did, a vision in my head showed a hand with a cloth coming toward my face. At that moment, I knew everything. I knew it had happened. I knew who. I knew when it had happened, and I knew why I never could remember. She confirmed it all in the next moments off what she was seeing and then added that my mother had been drugged as well so she couldn't uncover it either.

Apparently, he was putting some sort of a sleeping pill in her tea or water and giving it to her before going to bed. This is not surprising as he was prescribing her all sorts of medication even though he was an OB/GYN. Like me, if she suspected, there was no proof. As a doctor, he would go out on call in the middle of the night to deliver a baby. He would come home, maybe do something in the kitchen but would go to the bathroom across the hall, turn the light and fan on, close the door and come into my room. He never turned on my light and instead used this pen flashlight he always carried in his pocket. He used either ether or chloroform on me to keep me mostly knocked out. I say mostly because I was told he didn't want me completely out because he wanted me to "respond."

He was a pharmacist before he was a doctor, so whether he used his doctor access to get that chemical or made it himself, it doesn't matter. This went on for over a decade. My stepfather drugged my mother, drugged me, molested me in my sleep every week for over a decade. Everything now made sense. As horrific as that knowledge was, in the moments that followed that epiphany my energy became in alignment with my mind and body in a way I hadn't felt before instantaneously, as if my chakras buttoned up into place. I literally felt a snapping sensation from my root to my crown.

I physically felt like I got hit with the flu out of nowhere. This was resistance energy releasing. Within thirty minutes of getting off the phone I had a major headache. I don't get headaches. I tried to lay down, didn't help. Was up for about twenty minutes, then started vomiting. I don't vomit unless it is food or alcohol. I had neither. I vomited three different times over an hour. I then had really bad sweats and chills for six hours. When I went to bed the headache started going away. I don't remember my dreams hardly ever, but that night I had the most horrific dream, and I remembered the dream. It was so real I thought it was until I woke up and realized it wasn't. I dreamed my cats and dog were peeing and shitting everywhere. EVERYWHERE intentionally in my house.

I went through about eight days of an emotional crash. Horrified by how wrecked my spirit and body had been as a child growing up. The complete lack of empathy toward another human being, the depth of evil, horror, and deception incurred by this man against me. I was upset, crying, tired, and then raging. Repeating this cycle over and over before I started to come out of the fog. In the days after the discovery, I had a moment of despair feeling, like there was no one I could talk to about this. Again a voice yelled out the name of my cousin rather emphatically telling me to call her. In the moment, I was surprised by it, but in the moments after, it made a lot of sense.

When I called her, she told me her family always thought "something was going on there" and that as sorry as she was that this happened, she was not surprised by this information. She then further told me that my aunt had confronted my mother about it, and they had a major blow-up over it. My mother apparently refusing to believe anything was happening. When I told my brother, he immediately said it made sense. And then said, so that is what the big fight between mom and our aunt was about that led them to not speaking for years. The realization of why my mother was freaked out about why I had a UTI at fourteen and was screaming at me about having sex. With who I had no idea. I didn't have a boyfriend, and having sex with a boy didn't seem appealing at all. I just wanted the UTI pain to go away. My brother also remembered that.

My aura, my subconscious, and unconscious all had known. All my chakras were jacked up and had been. The fear looking at my door each night, hoping he wouldn't come through, was because he had been coming through all along. My fears that had been unsubstantiated for so long had now been uncovered as a horror far greater than I could have ever imagined. In fact, all of the other abuse encountered seemed irrelevant and insignificant in contrast. I am just not wired this way at a soul level. Even when you think about someone making a repeated action, choosing to make that action over and over with no remorse or care for another life—it is a depth of evil I wish on no one. Yet, there are millions of people that go through this awfulness. In fact, I will go into the topic of pedophilia deeper in the Conspiracy Theories section.

To complicate the depth of my shame and sadness, was a shift in the perception I had had of my mother with the realization that she failed to protect me at every turn. A woman who at the point of another family member confronting her that they believed there was a problem, that she made the choice … to do nothing. She used to call me her gift from God, and yet, at that moment and every moment forward, she chose not to protect that gift from God, and instead refused to believe it. Just refused. She didn't investigate further. She just decided she was not going to believe it at all. Therefore it wasn't happening. I remember at some point around sixteen or seventeen, at times she started being awake in the middle of the night. My brother had also moved back home at that time. She had stopped sleeping in the same bed as my stepfather because he snored. In retrospect, I wonder if this was her secretly trying to find a moment of catching him in the act because of her suspicions. Instead of this strong woman I had always looked up to with the strength of perseverance in the face of adversity, I now only saw a weak woman.

For me, I had to get to a place of forgiveness. This was easier because I did love my mom. And as much as I had been upset by new information,

I inherently felt sadness and compassion for her because she had been abused in all of this as well. To have to face the knowledge that their choice directly put their child in horrific danger is a hard thing to swallow for anyone. Even in the spirit world when you do that life review.

I now understood so many things. Why I even wouldn't allow my child as a baby to be alone in that man's presence. Why I never wanted to stay at their house as an adult. Why I used to energetically get the shakes and panic attacks at the thought of immersing myself back into his physical space. What my doctor was hinting at when at the age of twenty-three when she said she was concerned about the amount of scar tissue in my vaginal wall. Why I can't orgasm unless I am clenching tightly as if I am fighting against something. Why I have those horrific images in my head at times. Why and how I got that UTI. At this point, there had been too many synchronicities in play. Nothing was contradicting each other and only reaffirming things and the path I was on.

In order to come out of this horror, I had to sit in the other horrific knowledge that I had signed up at some point on a conscious level to go into this shitshow of a planetary experience in order to be part of the overall solution. Which means I signed up understanding that some horrific shit could go down. That going into the human plane meant that anything was on the table to happen that could wreak more than my soul, but my physical body. Well, it did. Fuck my life. Or at least this current one. Not that the other ones were probably all that great either. More crying and frustration with myself ensued. Holding my inner child a lot, broken at how much someone had broken me without my knowledge or consent and how it had impacted my personality and relationships.

A silver lining that occurred within forty-eight hours of this discovery was the indication that I had previously been a healer in a past life. Somehow the topic of hot hands came up in my discussion with my cousin. Apparently, hot hands or sweaty palms are a sign of a healer in a past life. The hotter the hands, the more lives of being a healer. I had never understood my hot hands. I just figured it was a hormonal imbalance or something. When that new clue clicked in synchronicity with me, a rage started burning inside me. If I have been a healer in a past life, then it technically is in my soul consciousness, which means, I can heal again. If that asshole fucked me, then I will fix myself. The other realization that hit me at this time was learning about chakras and energy and how it moves through the body. I go more in detail in the Healing Chapters on this stuff, but here is the general loop on how trauma works in conjunction with the body.

I previously indicated that your consciousness/higher self before you are born maps a blueprint of high-level experiences you agree to. Now I personally feel there are loopholes, and there are some things that are a miss on this blueprint concept. I see the experiences more like, I agree to a form of trauma. Some might agree to have this type of experience with a specific soul. But I don't necessarily agree that each person that rolls into your life was a soul contract you agreed to in this lifetime. This is where generational curses come into play and previous entity attachments from lifetimes ago that find you in a new lifetime. Additionally the reason why I don't resonate with the idea you agree to everything is because this whole experience of life on Earth, is all about choices. You have the choice to do this or do that. Even not choosing to do something is a choice in itself. Because choice is such a critical element, now layer in all the core people in your life, and realize that each one of them have their own blueprints and each one of them is operating in their own set of choices.

In my situation, my mother's choices rolled my brother and me into that experience. She had lots of other choices. She didn't have to marry this guy she met on a boat. So many things could have gone different ways. I also believe you make soul contracts with people that might not ever be fulfilled in this lifetime simply due to the choices you make. No one talks about unfulfilled soul contracts, almost as if that doesn't exist, but to me, they have to exist, or else everything is preplanned, and there is no element of choice at all. That isn't a line of thinking I can get behind. Do I believe I agreed to experience trauma, sure. That is part of the ascension plan. To break through the problems that one ego contributes to on this planet. We came into this planet to help fix it and help everyone evolve by being seeded in families with generational curses we had to clear. Because change within the current system of souls wasn't going to happen otherwise. The older Starseeds were tired and needed some fresh life infused on this Earth plane to tip the scales dramatically. But when I think of my own blueprint, there is absolutely nothing that resonates with me, nor has at any point in time for me to believe I intentionally designed in my blueprint to be drugged and molested by my stepfather for over a decade and then walk around for another few decades having amnesia about it. Nothing in my soul comes to that. In fact, there is an unsettling eerie stillness I do feel about it. Which is completely different than when I sit in a feeling of knowing with my claircognizance. As well as not feeling the same as when I get my confirmation energy shivers. I don't believe that we are all just here to have experiences and grow, or that it is all love and light. It is most certainly not all love and light. Additionally, every past life I am aware of has had me choosing to be in a difficult if not horrific situation because I believed I could make a positive change. These lives had nothing to do with the clearing of my karmic ties of ever being an abuser.

Some people can stay in that headspace, and good for them. We need people that can. But we also need people who are clear that it is not all love and light. There are many in the spiritual community that will lead you to believe that we are all of source (light). But there are contradictions to this idea. As I said before, we haven't put any really dark souls under regression to see what their souls say. Some regression therapists have noted that some people act as if it isn't to be talked about what happens to the really dark souls when they die. They are effectively led to a side door, and well, we don't speak about it. Think about yourself for a minute. If you were a soul actively in the growth and ascension process and you were told—you need to go in to be a mass murderer, does that resonate with you as something you would want to do? Something you think, sure why not. It doesn't add up. It's like making it to a certain level in a video game after many attempts at trying and being told, how about you go back to level 1? I don't think so. Even an actor playing a villain knows it is just a make-believe role.

It is because of this, along with other concepts on spirituality, that the possibility of a false matrix system and spiritual war (and some deep meditation) that I believe that not all of us are from the light source. That there is, in fact, a dark source, and there are souls that stem from that source that are put in play. The light sprang from the dark after all, why is it so hard to think that maybe there is a dark source? That it is a dark source creator and a light source creator that are at the heart of this overall spiritual dance of soul evolution or degradation. That certainly would fit the picture of the dichotomy of souls and the polarity that is overarching. A yin and a yang of souls.

Anyway, the blueprint knows what kind of experience, and therefore which chakras will be activated by the emotional/physical trauma. Those are all encoded as part of your DNA in your light-based consciousness. When you are born, the DNA you have encoded in your physical body correlates to the DNA of your consciousness for this lifetime. When those experiences occur, and you choose the predictable path and do not look to resolve them, your body energetically starts to send signals to the nearest chakras and creates resistance energy. This resistance energy cycles through the chakras which is connected to both your body and your aura and sends signals to the brain. The physical DNA markers are then activated within your physical body, and some form of disease or dis-ease begins to occur. Over time it continues to manifest until it causes your body enough strain you seek medical attention. To add to that, a poor diet works against the body, and to compound all of this, most of us are no longer grounded to the Earth which means, all the negative energy simply cycles back up through your body over and over.

In my case, I had some low back birth defects, but I had an auto-immune dis-ease in my low back discovered in my early thirties that had been flaring starting in my early twenties. When I read the book *The Emotion Code* in the Empath Chapter, this is why I screamed. The emotional and physical trauma I went through, essentially rocked all my chakras but the target was my root and sacral chakra. As a result, my DNA activated the marker (I actually do have a DNA marker for this dis-ease), and my body turned on itself creating physical trauma in my sacrum. My dis-ease festers and will continue until I resolve the issue in my aura, my mind, and then start healing my body. I go through how to heal yourself in all three areas in the Healing Chapters. This is a process I went through as a way to get off all my medication and physically heal myself from the dis-ease the trauma caused.

THE AKASHIC RECORDS TRAPS

Reviewing your Book of Life means you are going to look for some sort of trauma. It isn't a tool for you to go looking to identify with a past life that might have been more palatable for you than this one is, and you instead decide to start trying to live a parallel of a past life. You lived that lifetime—it is done. It is this lifetime you need to review and resolve and have new and different experiences. After all, you signed up for this, and what you don't learn in this life, you will repeat in the next one. The key is to not repeat the past.

The next trap is the emotional fallout from what you find. Let me be clear, it is expected for you to have some form of emotional reaction from the information you find. Even if this life hasn't been so bad, you may find something in your past that is. Something that maybe you don't even want to sit in the know on. Something you can be so ashamed and maybe even disgusted with your current self. So the key here is not to go looking for all your bad juju at once. Because you need to work on resolving one thing at a time emotionally. If you overload yourself with too many negative emotional scenarios to work through, it can put you into a mental state of depression and anxiety.

The Book of Life, while healing, invokes pain in that healing process. A necessary one, but painful still. The chances are overwhelmingly high you will find out information you might rather not have. But you don't break karmic cycles if you don't know what they are and if you don't tackle them head on in all its ugliness. Why is it important to break a karmic cycle? Simple, because if you don't learn the lesson or resolve it in this lifetime, you will repeat it in the next lifetime you reincarnate, and your future families will have to deal with your choices again. And when your body dies, and your light body is reconnected to your higher self in doing this lifetime of review, you will go, well, that was dumb.

CHAPTER 10

OTHER SPIRITS AND ENTITIES

While I covered the basics of being clairaudient earlier, I wanted to expand upon that further because it opens up another avenue of discussion. Are we the only light-based consciousnesses? Definitely not. Are we the most advanced? Not even close. We are ultimately getting to creationism in this book.

In New Age spirituality doctrines, you arrive at the notion that God or the ultimate Source Creator has been polluted in definition by man through religious dogma. Many gods noted before were actually just advanced humanoid races from elsewhere that came to Earth in different parts of history. There is no God in the sense of something that intentionally controls its creation. Source simply exists. In the beginning, light did come from darkness. Some say this was the Big Bang Theory. All consciousnesses come from Source. Source doesn't respond in the form of prayers (prayers are simply your energy put forth for your guides to engage with on your life path). It simply is something to connect to.

Source is our origin and where we feel the highest vibrations as a light-based consciousness. Our experiences are integrated to it in one large connecting web with other light-based spirits. It is hard to get to, but even who we would consider evil people in the world are still light-based consciousnesses. They simply vibrate at a substantially lower emotional frequency. We all are connected to Source, we all will return to Source, and thus we are all connected to each other. Obviously this concept directly conflicts with what I mentioned at the end of the previous chapter of a Light Source and a Dark Source. But we are going to move forward with the rest of this book under the assumption that we are all of the same Source.

When someone can "hear" someone/something else, it is because they are tuning in to a different brain wave frequency that another consciousness can communicate across. There is a lot of discussion about dimensions being planes of existence as well as dimensions being different intelligent levels of thinking and processing data. There are other conscious-based spirits. Some are said to be Angels, some are friends and family who have not incarnated again, some have chosen to stay in your realm until your death and new contracts can be made. Some are others from your older soul families on other planets. Both malevolent and benevolent entities are around us or can tune into certain frequencies around us. You probably would be quite frightened if you could see them all.

Everyone has at least one primary spirit guide they made a soul contract with that is with you before you are born and through your death transition as well. Their primary objective is to help in any way they can and keep you on track with your life path and blueprint. Sometimes it is in ways that might not seem helpful, but trust me, they are. When your life has gone off the rails, and you can't figure out why that is your spirit guide trying to tell you that you are on the wrong path and something needs to change. It is the uncomfortableness trying to shine a light on what needs to change. Some people have a large team of spirits assisting them. But your primary guide is with you through it all. This spirit is usually an entity you knew in some other existential experience you have had together.

Why can some people hear their guides better than others? Good question. Some people have always been able to tap into that frequency and leaned into it instead of shutting it down. Remember the kids who all had imaginary friends they would talk to? Now you start to think, wait a minute, maybe those imaginary friends weren't so imaginary after all. The reason why many can't hear is due to the Veil of Consciousness. It's where you lose all memory of your past life experiences as you cross over into a human body. Also it is the same veil you cross back over when you die. Others start to close up in childhood, around the age of eight or so.

Indigenous tribes for many centuries have used Shamans who routinely do meditations to tap into other frequencies to see what they can hear. Ever feel like your deceased friend or relative is in your brain telling you what you should do in a specific moment, and you hear their voice and their tone just as if they were still there today? Yeah, you are talking to them. Or rather, they are definitely talking to you.

When I looked back on my life, there were times they did come through and intervened in some pretty bad spots. I started realizing that the voice that was saying these brilliant sassy one-liners back at me when I would do dumb or funny stuff was actually male. When you hear yourself talk in your head, you know what your inner voice sounds like. This one was actually male. Wait a second here, who is this imposter in my head? Start paying attention to the deviations in your inner voice. Is it occasionally a different female voice? Once you start to hear, if you don't already, this is where you have to trust yourself. Trust your gut instinct. Not the thought the brain immediately engages onto to discredit it after the gut instinct thought, but the first intuitive thought that comes to you, and go with it.

How do you communicate with your guides? Start asking them questions and to send you clues or signs. You will be surprised at what synchronicities or interesting things start happening when you do. Also, when you ask for the name, let your brain go. Chances are, your spirit guide's name is not a common one. My guide's name I had never heard before he popped it out at me and just kept repeating it over and over until I said—okay, I got it, buddy. If a name doesn't come to you, then try a different day. Practice makes perfect, especially in areas that need to be developed more.

SPIRIT TRAP

Understand that a key fundamental in your spirit guides is that they will always be working to keep you on the right path, the path of love and light. If you EVER hear spirits telling you negative things, those are not your spirits, and you need to immediately get that under control. Your spirit guides are benevolent and here to help. Anything that does not resemble that for you, should be questioned. Schizophrenic individuals are people who have multiple low vibrational entities that tell them negative things. Not everything is all love and light. There is a dark side, so don't get sucked into it.

I discussed previously that Source wasn't something to pray to for help but instead something to connect with. Source is a connection to that ultimate feeling of home. Of love without judgment, of connection to every other consciousness that is connected to it. However, your spirit guides, on the other hand—they are the ones you ask for help. They are the ones you have a conversation with and say, "This is what I am going through. This is what I need. This is where I am struggling. What can you do to help? Please send me some clues so I can help myself." You would be surprised at what happens when you stop praying to a God that isn't listening, and instead having an honest conversation even if it feels one sided about your struggles to the spiritual entities that are trying to help you specifically on your path.

DEMONS AND ANGELS

Other types of dimensional entities are Demons and Angels. I have seen both. I know in both of those instances what I saw, and it defied all reality. I saw a demon through the eyes of a boyfriend who tried to strangle me when his entire eyes went black. I saw an angel defy time and space to wake me up from a horrific dream of being raped by the devil at eighteen. Other people have seen other things as well, from angels to demons, to orbs, magical creatures, and more. How many times have you watched shows about ghost hunting or heard stories from friends about experiences of seeing a ghost or haunted house? What situations have you encountered that you know you are dealing with some low vibrational entity where you felt like there was a demon in your midst? What in your life have you encountered that you know shouldn't be viable, but you know what you saw? I am sure you have a story somewhere in there. So many people have moments they can't explain but they were very real to them in what they saw or heard.

If you ever dabble in Aleister Crowley books, you will realize the spiritual plane is to be taken seriously as demons do exist.

CHAPTER 11

NEW AGE SPIRITUALITY

Knowing that this was not only not my first life, but I have had lots of past lives, led me into a new area of discovery. I had gone down the intuitive path and came to an understanding, and it led to an empath encountering trauma as part of our blueprints to be receivers of trauma but then breakers of the karmic chains that bind and perpetuate more trauma. Which led me to say, but why? This then led me to the discovery of Starseeds.

I never said exactly how old we are as light-based consciousnesses. There is some dispute that all consciousnesses were created at the same time. They simply have had experiences in different places. In that line of thinking, that means that we are actually billions of years old, and most of us have had millions of years' experience on other star systems. That is a bit to take in. There are some who believe some souls are older than others. That Source continues to create new light-based consciousnesses to experience life, and these are strategically placed on planets with a 3D experience. If they evolve from a light-based consciousness, then they essentially "ascend" to higher levels of dimensional consciousness.

When I stumbled on Starseeds in parallel with researching reincarnation, I felt relief. This made sense. Are you someone who never quite knew where home was? Do you ever feel like you don't really fit in, even if it looks differently from an outsider's perspective? Do you ever look up at the stars and feel an unexplained connection to somewhere else? Ever feel like you have a mission you just aren't sure what it is? For me, it was the feeling like I never knew where home was and feeling like I had some sort of a mission to fulfill that I wasn't quite sure what that was. Nowhere feeling like I think home should feel. That home simply equated to wherever I was at the moment.

Starseeds are spirits who originally came from other star systems who incarnate on Earth to help with the spiritual evolution process to move humankind forward. Especially because humans have regressed several times. When I say spiritual evolution, these are spirits with advanced knowledge reincarnating for a specific purpose to add to the collective knowledge base. There is some dispute as to what went wrong with the human race as to why there was an influx of Starseeds. What is not in dispute is that after the atomic bomb in the 1940s, a huge influx came to Earth to try and ensure that never happened again. It is referred to as "The Call." Many people in regression therapy say, "I heard the call and knew I had to come to help," or "I knew I could help or was needed." Dolores Cannon writes extensively about Starseeds and the waves of them. It is tricky as a result to determine the first timers vs the old timers. What you will read interchangeably is that Starseeds are Lightworker. However, Starseeds have actually been coming to Earth for quite a while.

At this point, this is how my thinking went. I am an advanced spirit that originated from somewhere else. I came into this shitshow of a planet to help the planet evolve to where it needed to be. And when I die, this won't be my last go-round either.

This made sense. I mean, I even asked myself out loud to confirm. "Am I a Starseed?" Those energy chills cycled through my body. "I am a Starseed." Energy chills again. Throughout my research, that was one of my queues for confirmation. If I got full-body energy chills when asking questions out loud or confirming something. It was a little eerie that this energy transference occurred in those moments—confirmation of something I had never given that kind of thought to. I was really old. It almost is an unfathomable concept to think of being a million years old.

There are a lot of terms you will find in researching Starseed—Indigos, Rainbow, Crystal Children, Lightworkers, Walk-Ins. These are waves of types of Starseeds, and they have specific attributes linked to them. In short, what this means is your spirit came from somewhere else. Maybe recently, maybe a very long time ago. The waves noted above are more characteristic based. Not everyone in that way is a newbie.

Cameron Day wrote extensively on all of these topics and was one of the people whose writings are what helped me link things together. He actually wrote a post years ago as to why he stepped away from being a lightworker. No matter what you ultimately get to, I think, at a minimum, look into his work as stepping-stones in your research.

THE STARSEED/LIGHTWORKER TRAP I

Something early in this discovery was bugging me, and it would take a little while to figure it out. How could I be a Starseed that just came in this wave if I have past lives on this planet? Further research led me to that I was indeed a Starseed, but there is a crew of us that have been doing this for a very long time. Additionally, I stumbled upon another answer in Cannon's work called imprinting lives. You might be a first timer, but in order to be able to handle the dense 3D experience of Earth you have to imprint other lifetimes in your etheric soul. In regression therapy, it can get tricky to get past those imprint lifetimes to uncover the ones before that, but it can be done.

There are Starseeds that did primarily come into Earth over the last seventy years, but there is also a large crew that came in a long time ago that go back to the time of Atlantis. We get to Atlantis later. The trap is thinking that we are all relatively new to this experience and therefore have no past life karma tied to us that we need to clear. Even if you have imprints, you have to clear the energetic residue tied to them. Beyond that, it doesn't matter if you identify with a certain wave of Starseed, just that you lean into your consciousness being really old and evolved. The idea is that we hold more genetic memory in our etheric layers due to millions of years of evolutionary process and rising in frequency. If you completely buy into the theory you are a newer Starseed, you need to go into Akashic to confirm. Otherwise, you just fell into a trap that has you not looking at past lives on Earth and trauma you need to clear and effectively trying to spiritually bypass the process.

LIGHTWORKER TRAP 2

The other lightworker trap is the individuals you think are on the side of the light but are not. They are deceivers, and thus why your individual discernment is important. Not everyone masquerading as a Lightworker is, in fact, working for good. I personally feel that some of the Lightworker stuff you see advertised is a bit of fluff.

LIGHTWORKER TRAP 3

If you are a Starseed, then you have already ascended at least once before in an evolutionary cycle. So don't get caught up too much in the Ascended Master topics in the Starseed conversations. You technically are an Ascended Master already. You just forgot and are doing it all over again. No one would have agreed to come here in this density to go through the harsh experiences here if they hadn't already gone through at least one cycle of ascension. So when you see the mentions of Ascended Masters, be careful here.

Buddha, while awesome for all his Zen teachings, we still need to recap. He sat under a tree for forty-nine days straight and had snails crawl on his head. While the teachings say he found enlightenment, if you go back and look again, what Buddha found was zero-point energy. Basically, I am not participating in this game on Earth. With Jesus, I discuss further on in Conspiracy Theories the existence of Jesus. So when Jesus comes into play in the Ascended Masters discussions, I get a little nervous. When they bring in Shiva, I get even more nervous as Shiva was an extraterrestrial. I mean, that is pretty obvious. I don't really like to look up to the Ascended Master version within New Age, because I think it can still be deceiving. Like we are looking to reach the enlightenment of others that we don't possess. When the truth is, we do possess it. We have ascended before. In the end, we are light-based bodies of consciousness having a human experience.

As to what our role is in the planetary evolution, go looking for that on your own and see what you come to and what resonates with you. There are channelings by people that are posted in written and video form that discuss Starseeds and their connections back to their soul group of origin. When you are feeling down during this journey, sometimes reading or listening to those channelings make you feel better and give you a little hope.

In realizing spirits have come from different star systems and were dense physical bodies at different points in a different place in the universe I found information on Syrians, Orions, Arcturians, Pleiadieans, and a couple of others. But that is just a drop in the bucket in the types of spirits incarnating on Earth. If there are billions of universes and billions of stars in those universes and billions of planets orbiting those stars, then there are an unbelievable amount of possible origin stories. Star Wars allegedly was based on the Orion Wars from millions of years ago. Go look into that. There is more, a lot more.

So if you didn't connect the dots above, then let me be clear … we are the aliens. Our spirits are of alien origin and linked to another or multiple stars systems, galaxies, and universes. If that isn't enough, then think of it this way, we are the only living creatures on Earth that don't integrate ourselves with the land, instead of destroying it in the process of living on it. We don't live in harmony with the Earth even though the Earth gives us everything we need. Water to drink, air to breathe, food to eat, and before industrial destruction, a beautiful planet to live on. No other animal on Earth destroys each other or the Earth like humans do. So while everyone is looking for aliens elsewhere, the truth is, we are the aliens.

ITEM OF CONFLICTION

There are references to the influx of Starseeds over the last seven decades, of them being 144,000. A number that was first indicated as the 144,000 tribes of Israel in the Bible in Luke and Revelations. In Revelations, the prophecy is that before the end of the world, it is noted that the twelve tribes of Israel, which equated to 144,000 people would return before the rapture. Everyone in the Starseed sphere believes they are one of the 144,000. But remember, things are fluid. And from what I have seen in the Awakening community, there are a lot more than 144,000. So where I eventually got to is, maybe at one time it was thought 144,000 could get it done, but at this point, it is several billion spread out all over the globe.

In New Age spirituality, the Galactic Federation is a collaboration of alien races that basically oversee the activities of Earth with the understanding they are not to directly interfere in what is happening on the planet. The GF had the ability to see into future timelines of the Earth. After Atlantis sunk, they saw the timeline of nuclear technologies and where we were headed with the planet. So they came up with a plan and sent out a call to all beings and star systems in the universe asking for volunteers. Out of billions of beings, only 144,000 were willing to volunteer. It was explained like this: Another planet with substantial ripple effects into everyone's star system is in peril if we don't do something. The assignment will be to reincarnate into human bodies for many thousands of human lifetimes, under a veil of forgetting who you really are, your spirit will be traumatized in most lifetimes, and because of restrictions that will be in play, anything is fair game. That means, you can be beaten, sexually abused, starved, neglected, and etc, etc, pretty much your worst-case scenario for spirits who have already evolved past all this nonsense and spirits who are used to a different experience. Thousands of lifetimes, your spirit will be trashed, but if we don't, then we all have something to risk.

SEXUALITY

This section could have gone in a couple different places in this book. But I chose to put it here because I have seen a disconnect within the spiritual community. The disconnect is the people who still cling to their traditional view of man and woman. That transgender and homosexuality is part of the Cabal's plan for the denigration of marriage. Let me tell you what I think.

That's complete bullshit.

It is interesting to see someone who is anti-LGBTQ change their views when someone they love and care for is. That presents a dichotomy within oneself of standing for a preconceived belief they were taught versus standing in the light with the one they have loved for a long time. The idea they could lose this person they love over an ideal they held on to.

When I look at different types of missions a spirit could have in this quest, I think one of the hardest assignments a Starseed can take on, is one of being a spirit who identifies as a female or male on gender principles, but put into a physical human body that does not mirror that concept. The experience that spirit has in the stretching of one's mind and what constitutes the emotions that come with that, the love or the hate energy they receive as a result. For me, these are some of the toughest of the Starseeds. Their mission is not just to have that experience themselves, but to specifically hold themselves in the light and illustrate that gender itself does not define sexuality, nor does it necessarily define the true gender of a spirit. For our spirits were born in a different time, a different star system, and it was associated with a gender, so we retain that identity in the DNA collection within our spirit.

I understand what it is like to have an identity crisis. I understand what it is like to look in the mirror and say—I don't know who that person I am looking at is, but it is not "me." Not the real me. This is how I felt for the first few years after I had my son. I don't know who that woman is, but I know I don't like her, and I know that is not me. My self-esteem and self-image were totally in the trash. I had been a certain way for thirty years, and now, this person in no way resembled the person I identified with the first thirty years.

People that are transgender are like all of us who came in. We forgot our purpose due to the veil of consciousness being manipulated and forgetting who we are. As a result, non-CIS individuals are here to break through those barriers on what is perceived as acceptance and love. Changing the view to understand that love is fluid. Identify if you are a spirit that holds a different gender within your DNA encoded aura and show the world how one bridges that gap emotionally and mentally to defy what constitutes one's gender, one's sexuality, and the feminine and masculine energies that all intertwine. I will be honest—it's a garbage assignment I wouldn't want to take, which is why I say these are some of the strongest spiritual warriors we have.

The other part about the destruction of the family is where I get pissed. Because LGBTQ have absolutely no weight in the game on the destruction of the family unit by far. The destruction of the family unit is solely at the hands of negative programming regimes and is primarily rooted in how low vibrational men have treated women and children. The breakdown of the family unit is done when a parent abuses another parent or abuses their children. Plain and simple. How many cases of LGBTQ individuals can you say meet that criteria compared to the traditional male/female ones? I can only think of one compared to the billions in the traditional paradigm.

CHAPTER 12

SACRED GEOMETRY

After I told someone I was learning about numerology, she mentioned I look into Sacred Geometry. I made a joke about being terrible in geometry in school, so why would I even want to learn about it. Sacred Geometry has its root in creationism and the building blocks of the universe. The basics of Sacred Geometry is that everything in the universe is made using mathematical proportions and specific geometric shapes. These shapes can be seen in everything in nature, art, architecture, music, religion, and more.

The specific shapes that meet the criteria for Sacred Geometrical shapes are called Platonic solids after the Ancient Greek scholar Plato who documented these findings, even though they have been in use since the dawn of time. A Platonic solid is a polyhedron where all its faces are congruent (identical in shape and size), regular (all angles equal and all sides equal) polygons, and where the same number of faces meet at every vertex.

There are five shapes that meet this criteria: tetrahedron, hexahedron, octahedron, dodecahedron, and icosahedron. According to Plato, each shape corresponds to one of the five elements: earth, fire, water, air, and ether. These solids are the building blocks upon which organic matter are created.

While I didn't study Sacred Geometry in great depth as it wasn't something I knew I was meant to spend a great deal of time on; I highly suggest watching the YouTube video by Spirit Science called The Sacred Geometry Movie. It gives you the entire layout of Sacred Geometry in a way that is easy to understand and how it applies to everything. They actually have quite a few other videos that might be helpful on your journey, so I suggest exploring those. I found myself afterward thinking, I get it, but how does it come to life, so to speak. What could be an example that shows you how this works and comes together without saying, just look around you at the universe? Most of the explanations or renderings are one dimensional, and thus, I wanted a 3D example of bringing it to life.

I found my answer in the documentary The Code with Marcus du Sautoy. It walks you through different elements of how mathematics is the secret code of the universe and where it is found. In the documentary he introduced The Bubble Man, and it was this specific part of the documentary where this man blows bubbles, essentially showing you how spheres work and combine. Now in Sacred Geometry when forming the seed of life or the flower of life, it starts with spheres. It shows the overlapping of the spheres and how the repeating pattern works.

However, it was in this bubble demonstration that a lightbulb went off. You see, a sphere is the most efficient shape in relation to using the least amount of surface area/energy. When two spheres combine, you see where they overlap. But in practical application, when two spheres combine, they don't overlap, they in fact combine where they meet to make a flat plane, still using the basic principle of using the least amount of space. As The Bubble Man continued his demonstration, you could see where even triangles would form in places where multiple spheres had overlapped. He could even interject air into this massive 3D geometric shape he was building and create more shapes within it. This was the moment I saw Sacred Geometry come to life before my eyes. The documentary was great, and I don't want to take anything away from it, but the bubble demonstration gripped me hard. If you want to learn about the building blocks of life, then Sacred Geometry is an avenue to explore.

CHAPTER 13

CROP CIRCLES/LEY LINES/MEGALITHIC/ NEOLITHIC STRUCTURES

U p to this point, the topics have been either metaphysical or theoretical in nature. But now, we are going to start connecting the spiritual plane to the tangible Earth/human plane—because it is all connected.

CROP CIRCLES

Crop circles have been reported all over the globe and are an area of debate. While some people claim to be the creators of crop circles, scientists have studied various crop circles, and researchers can tell the difference between man-made crop circles and crop circles of unknown origin based on how the stalks in the field are broken. In conclusion, there are quite a few of unknown origin.

If you look at a lot of these crop circles, what you see is a picture. If we were to communicate with extraterrestrial life, it would be through Sacred Geometry and mathematical principles. When you look at these 1D/2D visual representations and then morph them into a Sacred Geometry 3D representation, there is a different message. We just aren't smart enough to figure out what it says.

However, there was a crop circle in 2002 in Hampshire, England. A university mathematician was actually able to deduce it was a binary code message next to a picture of an alien. The interpretation: *Much pain but still time. Believe. There is good out there. Beware the bearers of false gifts and their broken promises. We oppose deception. Conduit closing.*

While crop circles have also popped up near ley lines and other areas, when you look at the mathematical precision these had to have in order to be created, it is beyond what we can do today with any technology. Whether you believe in them or not, you have to admit that there is something odd about them.

LEY LINES

Ley lines are the Earth's energetic planetary grid lines (not latitude or longitude). When you look at where ley lines connect throughout the world and then overlay many ancient structures, it presents an entirely new insight into the Earth's placement of various megalithic structures. It is thought that ley lines are associated with paranormal activity. The idea is that these structures all over the world work together in a planetary grid system of energy somehow. If you look at the Earth and the primary ley lines, you see synchronicities in play.

Well-known paranormal activity throughout the globe occurs on key lines or where they intersect. Bermuda Triangle? It is a vortex of several ley lines. Devils' Triangle near the Asian coast is the same. The Mothman Prophecies based on the Mothman sightings in West Virginia were also on a ley line. The Pyramids? One of the main intersections. In fact, the idea is that the Pyramids might have been what energized the grid. Many of the ancient ruins are also coordinated on ley lines as well. Stonehenge? Same. Some believe that where ley lines intersect, they actually form portals to other dimensions or to other places on Earth. Many of the odd and unusual paranormal sightings and disappearances also occur along ley lines.

Beyond the ley lines, there is also the idea of a false white light grid matrix. Essentially that there is an overlay upon our normal energetic grid system, and it is in some sort of a lockdown state. You may see people talk about working on repairing the grid system in the astral realm. That would be worked to destroy the old matrix webbing and fix it with a new grid. The understanding is that with various cataclysmic events, the planetary grid system is severely damaged.

MEGALITHIC AND NEOLITHIC STRUCTURES

Most people are aware of the most well-known megalithic structures, such as Stonehenge and the Egyptian Pyramids. But there are megalithic structures all over the world. The below is a list of just a few of them but all are built with a combination of astronomical positions with the stars, using technology we can't explain and have acoustical and energy reso-nator components.

+ Prambanan Temple, Indonesia
+ Borobudur, Indonesia
+ Medinet Habu, Egypt
+ Abu Simbel, Egypt
+ The Colossi Of Memnon, Egypt
+ Karnak, Egypt
+ Philae Temples, Egypt
+ Egyptian Pyramids
+ Mahabodhi Temple, India
+ Angkor Wat, Cambodia
+ Temple of Hephaestus, Greece
+ Ness Of Brodgar, Scotland
+ Stonehenge, England
+ Machu Picchu, Peru
+ Chan, Peru
+ Nazca Lines, Peru—The Nazca Lines in southern Peru are a group of pre-Columbian geoglyphs etched into desert sands.
+ San Agustín Archaeological Park, Columbia—The park contains the largest collection of religious monuments and megalithic sculptures in Latin America and is considered the world's largest necropolis.
+ Chichen Itza, Mexico
+ Tulum, Mexico
+ Tikal, Guatemala
+ Caracole, Belize

Now let's discuss the two common ones. The Great Pyramid was originally told to us that they were temples that housed ancient Egyptian kings. Except that is a problem when they didn't find any tombs. What they did find, and reverse engineered is that the Great Pyramid was some sort of a free energy generator. Either globally or possibly for remote energy consumption, and it was the primary source on the planet. It is assumed that the top of the pyramid actually had either a gold plate or a large crystal on it. The chemical residue they found in the great pyramid indicated they were using hydrogen inside the pyramid to generate energy. They also determined that the Nile River used to run directly underneath the Pyramid, which is the initial energy source to make the pyramid work. In generating this energy, the pyramid also vibrates energetically and then resonates at a certain frequency.

Michael Tellinger did research on these sites. When you look at them from a topical view, he determined that the Egyptian pyramids and the immediate surrounding area are identical to what we have developed with macro processors today. Literally, it is a like-to-like match. Just on an enormous scale and done using basic Earth elements.

The other issue with the Great Pyramid is the idea that humans built them. The Ancient Egyptians documented in their hieroglyphics that they had a slave force. What is incorrectly assumed is that the slave force was, in fact, building these pyramids. The glyphs don't illustrate that. What they were actually doing was mining for gold. The pyramids are associated with the Egyptians due to their location. The truth is, they can't carbon date the pyramids because it is made of limestone, which is not organic matter, so they don't really know how old they are. Scientists just made predictive assumptions.

The spirituality belief is that the Egyptian pyramids, along with other pyramids around the globe, were actually built a very long time ago by an Ancient Builder Race. A race of beings who came to planets and established grid systems and energy portals. When you look further into the pyramids, the architecture was done with such mathematical precision that it faces true North and the bricks that make up the pyramid have various interlocking sections to them, as well as precision-cut lines that even our best technology today and geologists are not able to replicate. They tried using one of the most durable cranes to move the bricks, not only did they have difficulty moving the medium-sized bricks, but they could also not move them slowly enough to ensure the precision of placement. They also know the quarry the limestone was taken from but don't know how they could have transported it.

So how did they before the time of the pulley construct these pyramids? Using mathematical precision that was not possessed at that time? Additionally, they found that the stones have interlocking pieces that appear to have been melded together. We don't even know how to do that today. The only way the pyramids could have been built was with some form of telekinesis-type abilities using levitation and laser like cutting technology.

They have discovered more pyramids now all over the Earth with the use of underground penetrating radar, as well as discovering ancient cities buried under the Earth and the sea. A pyramid was just discovered in Russia when they drained a lake. They found an underground city off the Mediterranean coast with massive statues. Apparently in China, they have also found another group as well. There is even a pyramid that is fully covered in greenery, and the Chinese government doesn't allow exploration of it.

When you look at Stonehenge, they determined that it functioned as a solar and lunar calendar or clock as one function. Michael Tellinger did a topical view of it and showed how Stonehenge mirrors a resonator energy device, and the sound resonating inside does so with symmetrical interference patterns. Sound creates magnetic fields, and moving magnetic fields creates electricity. In Angkor Wat, the structure was determined to have various sound frequency resonating chambers as well.

Further in Mr. Tellinger's research, he also found other sites being energy resonators. What is fascinating though, is he also then linked gothic structures and obelisks around the world as energy generators. Churches, for example, are one big energy generator, and you usually have that steeple on top, focusing the energy upward. The energy of the people inside then focuses upward to somewhere. Stadiums are often built on ley lines, and they too generate an enormous amount of energy. The question is, where is the energy going? When we congregate in a given area and then we emit a lot of energy, it all goes upward to the planetary grid matrix, or even further. Our roads are infrastructure to help further channel energy to these sources. Some people say that we are being harvested—our energy, at least for other alien races, is consumption. Possibility. But it does make you think. Something seems amiss here, yes?

Another interesting fact is that the gothic structures are all designed with specific acoustical properties. The basics of architecture and engineering with this paradigm are associated with the Freemason's work. In the 1700s, the Catholic Church and the Freemasons had a major split with the Church, calling the Freemason's heretics. But were they really or did they possess ancient information handed down from advanced civilizations with respect to architecture and acoustical sound? Most stories of Freemasons are rooted in conspiracy theories and secret societies going back to thousands of years. So there are a lot of rabbit holes on this topic.

Once you start researching these ancient sites, you find that there is no logical explanation other than, more advanced humanoid extraterrestrial life has been on this planet way before we thought humans existed, and with technology we currently don't possess and with mathematical and scientific knowledge we also don't understand how to use them effectively. Is it really that much of a stretch to think that there is all sorts of intelligent life in the universe and has been for eons? It certainly is not what we have been told or led to believe. We scratch our heads when we find skeletal remains that are 100,000 years old. Scientists can't make the leap other than an evolution theory to figure out how we have gone through five different human DNA types. It seems that something about our history on our planet is amiss.

CHAPTER 14

ASTROLOGY

You cannot go down these rabbit holes without running into astrology—from tarot to sacred geometry, to consciousness, and that we are a billion years old, birth charts, numerology, mathematical computations in relation, to star systems we see from the ground.

Astrology is a pseudoscience of studying the movements and relative positions of planets, moons, stars, and suns. Mostly in relation to planet Earth and the impacts of alignments and electromagnetic pulls and their direct impacts on humans and terrestrial events. Astrology can be found going back at least a millennium illustrated in caves, paintings, and ancient cultures' calendars. Astrology was used to predict when to plant crops and when seasons would shift. Many cultures, including the Maya, Chinese, Hindus, and Egyptians, have attached importance to astronomical events and developed methodologies for predicting Earth events from celestial observations.

The current system of astrology traces its roots to 19th–17th century BC in Mesopotamia (which is currently the oldest civilization in Earth's history we can reliably trace back to). Mesopotamia's influence then spread to Ancient Greece, Rome, Central and Western Europeans as well as the Arab world. But astrology, being broken down to a mathematical science in understanding the exact rotation spins and orbits and duration of orbital cycles of planets in our solar system using geometrical models, was originally mapped out by the famous mathematician Claudius Ptolemy. He drew on ancient Babylonian texts as well as Greek in formulating his data. The same precision calculations are used today for active astrologers.

Current astrology is often associated with horoscopes that explain aspects of a person's personality and predict significant events in their lives based on the positions of celestial objects at given points in time.

Although the Zodiac remains the basis of the system used in astronomy, the term and the names of the twelve Zodiac signs today are mostly associated with horoscopes. The Zodiac signs are distinct from the constellations associated with them because the sun is not in each constellation for the same amount of time. The zodiacal signs are an abstraction from the physical constellations. The path of the sun passes through thirteen constellations recognized by ancient Babylonian, Greek, and Roman astronomers. Because the Babylonians had a twelve-month lunar calendar, they chose twelve and divided the year up evenly. The thirteenth named Ophiuchus was left out. Additionally the Earth has rotated on its axis since the original charting of constellations, so there is some debate on whether the old astrology signs should even apply anymore.

Ancient humans very much relied on the stars in our solar system as well as documenting that their gods came from the stars. You can look into probably any ancient indigenous tribes, and you will find stories telling of their "gods" descending from the heavens/sky/stars. The Egyptian pyramids are in alignment with Orion's belt. We also know the Giza plateau is perfectly aligned to both N/S/E/W compass points as well as being the geographical center of all the landmass on Earth. Another interesting fact is that the number sequence in the latitude of the Great Pyramid is also the exact match to the speed of light in a void. People have tried to debunk this as a mere coincidence, but all their arguments are rooted in the idea that humans are really only a few thousands years old, and so there was not that kind of advanced intelligence.

The Hopi tribe of North America lived in the northeastern part of Arizona and built their three mesas to align with the three stars of Orion's Belt. The pyramids in Teotihuacan in Mexico are aligned to Orion. We also know the Mayans were masters at astrology and placed their temples to align with star systems in the sky. The Mayan pyramid of the sun is perfectly aligned with the star cluster Pleiades. In fact, if you look at all the major temples on Earth, they all mention sky gods in their history, along with being aligned to star constellations in the sky as a representation of where their sky gods were from.

One of the most interesting things regarding Astrology is birth charts. The position of the planets at the exact time of your birth. The outputs that result from a birth chart can be quite uncanny as they provide the basis for your individuality, relationships, and life purpose. Add to the concept of numerology where you were intentionally born at a certain point of time that maps back to your blueprint and your sun sign horoscope indicators on personality traits. Even twins will have slightly different birth charts because they are born at different times. Astrology ties into tarot, horoscopes, birth charts, and more.

Regarding horoscopes, most of what is out there is fluff. But there are some astrologists that seriously are looking at the alignment of the planets and when and where and for how long and what those things indicate and for each sun sign. Your sun sign indicates your personality, your moon sign is the soul behind your identity, your rising sign is how you express yourself or approach life, all of which work together to form the basis of you. While most people do feel in alignment with their sun sign, for others, the moon sign and rising sign are more prevalent factors. Additionally, if you were born on a cusp of a sign, you often will have some traits from the sun sign on the opposite side of that cusp.

I don't get into Astrology specifics much because, to be honest, it is quite vast. You literally have a lot to study between what each planet indicates, position in rotation, moons and their positions, etc. Much more mathematical and predictive work than I desire to do. An astrologist can also do modeling of what your current planetary alignment looks like and the indications of it. A really good one can do predictive analysis on when the future challenges will be. There are lots of books out there to explore this topic further if you choose.

ASTRONOMY

Astronomy is the science that applies mathematics, physics, and chemistry in an effort to explain the origin of those objects and phenomena and their evolution that originate outside Earth's atmosphere. Think NASA. I mention it here so you know the difference between astronomy and astrology.

CHAPTER 15

TAROT

You also can't stumble down this path without tarot popping up. For many of us, this was part of the entry path to our Awakenings. But tarot creeps a lot of people out. I get it. That's why I chose to bury it a bit further down in the chapters. Out of everything in this journey that I have read or discovered, tarot cards still have an element of simply just, unexplainable magic. In a way, I can't even understand how the energy transfers to the cards and how the cards find their way to the place and order they need to be in. But they work.

I was nineteen when I had my tarot cards read for the first time. In a back room of a coffee shop at night by an engineering student who read them for fun. At the time, I didn't know a ton about tarot other than somehow they had predictive abilities. It seemed weird to me, but whatever. He had told me, "The cards don't play." He was right. Even when I think the cards might be wrong, usually after pondering on it for a while, the connection reveals itself. I have often done my cards and marveled at how it works.

As he went through and did his bit, I got creeped out in a way I had never been creeped out before. I felt like this guy was in my mind, digging into crevices that I only knew about. While I was relatively calm throughout this process, I walked away internally shaken for a spell. He nailed stuff. I have no idea how he nailed me, my past, etc. And the immediate future stuff all came true. How the fuck did that guy do that? I ended up picking up a deck of cards that summer. It is a deck I still have, and one that no one else has ever touched.

After realizing that I was an intuitive, one of the first ways you learn to work on improving your intuition is to start reading tarot cards. In researching tarot, what I found is that there are a lot of things that interweave into it, but it all centers around energy and a series of deductions mathematically that have already been determined for each card. The tuning in to a person mentally and receiving feedback on that person's signals through space and time, implanting it on the cards and then having the cards fall as they may.

There are a lot of different tarot card decks these days, many of them online. I have an Oracle deck and the Ryder Waite deck, which is the standard deck. The Oracle deck is a bit more mystical, and the book of interpretations that comes with it is amazing. The Ryder Waite deck is what most people at least start with, or the one they are most familiar with. Here is a rundown on how the standard tarot decks work to compile data to form an answer. I personally think BiddyTarot.com has the best interpretations of the cards if you are just learning to read.

Tarot cards use both numbers (Roman) that have properties of numerology, as well as categories of the Zodiac, which indicate earth, fire, water, air signs that correlate to them. Each card corresponds to a number that has a specific indication type, and each card type is associated with an earth element.

+ Cups (element = water): Emotions, creativity, intuition, relationships
+ Pentacles (element = earth): Material wealth, money, career, manifestation
+ Swords (element = air): Communication, truth, intellect, thoughts
+ Wands (element = fire): Inspiration, energy, enthusiasm
  1 – (Aces) New beginnings, opportunity, potential
  2 – Balance, partnership, duality
  3 – Creativity, groups, growth
  4 – Structure, stability, manifestation
  5 – Change, instability, conflict
  6 – Communication, cooperation, harmony
  7 – Reflection, assessment, knowledge
  8 – Mastery, action, accomplishment
  9 – Fruition, attainment, fulfillment
  10 – Completion, end of a cycle, renewal

The Major Arcana Tarot cards represent the life lessons, karmic influences, and the themes that are currently influencing your life and your spirit's journey in this lifetime on the path to enlightenment. When a Tarot reading is predominantly made up of Major Arcana cards, you are experiencing life-changing events that will have long-term effects.

The Suit of Cups deals with the emotional level of consciousness and is associated with love, feelings, relationships, and connections. They indicate you are thinking with your heart more than your head. Cups are associated with the element of water. Water is fluid, agile, and "in flow" but also powerful and formative. The element of water is feminine and symbolic of fluidity, feelings, and emotions, intuition, relationships, healing, and cleansing. It is receptive, adaptable and flowing. In a deck of playing cards, Cups correspond to Hearts.

The Suit of Pentacles deals with the physical or external level of consciousness (ego, self-image) and thus mirrors situations of your health, finances, work, and creativity as well as material aspects of life including work, business, trade, property, money, and other possessions. They indicate what we make of our external surroundings; how we create it, transform it, and grow it. Pentacles is associated with the element of earth. Earth is grounded, stable, supportive, tangible, and fertile. It is a feminine element that is receptive; it takes in nutrients and light energy and then uses it to sustain the life that grows from it. In a deck of playing cards, Pentacles correspond to Diamonds.

The Suit of Swords indicate the quality of mind in your present thoughts, attitudes, and beliefs. Swords symbolize the fine balance between intellect and power and how these elements can be used positively or negatively. Because of this, Swords must be balanced by spiritual awareness (Wands) and feelings (Cups) to have the most positive outcome. Swords are associated with the element of air. Air is intangible and unseen, but is also in constant movement even when it feels still. The element of air relates to knowledge, action, power, and change. It is a masculine energy that can lead by force and power, even though it remains unseen. In a deck of playing cards, Swords correspond to Spades.

The Suit of Wands is associated with the spiritual level of consciousness and mirror what is important to you at the core of your being and how they drive you: your energy, spirituality, inspiration, determination, strength, intuition, creativity, personality, and enthusiasm. Wands are associated with the element of fire. Fire is a masculine element and reflects the drive and willpower of the masculine energy. In a deck of playing cards, Wands correspond to Clubs.

THE TAROT TRAP

The tarot trap is twofold. First, it is love. As humans, many of us are on a constant quest to seek love, feel love, receive, and give love. But we often get mired in deception, unrealistic expectations, and challenges in that quest. But it doesn't mean most of us stop desiring it. The reason why I say love is the trap in tarot is because the amount of scenarios that can be in play in a general reading for, say Aries or all singles, is that it is just way too broad. If you want a love reading, then you need to have one that is either specific to you and your current situation, or you need to review one that is specific to Aries Singles or Aries in Relationships. Would a twenty-year-old be in the same experiences that a forty-year-old would? Probably not. If you want to know what is going on in your love life, you need someone reading specifically on your current energy.

The second trap is taking a generalized reading that doesn't resonate with you and discounting either the tarot or the reader as nonsense. Generalized readings are just that, generalized. They are good for an overall theme or idea or possibly a specific problem that you might face. That means not everyone will resonate with what the reader pulled or how they interpret the cards. Doesn't mean the reader was wrong. Just that the reading didn't apply to you. Take what does, discard the rest, or go watch a different reader.

If you are looking for an intuitive of any type to assist you, then I cannot stress enough to look for someone running their own show. Those are the ones you should trust the most out of the gate when looking. From there, take what you feel in looking at their stuff and if they feel right for you. If you are looking for perfection, then you must be forgetting perfection is something that rarely exists in anything. It isn't about perfection. It is more about percentages and does someone seem viable. Understand psychics, including tarot readers, see possibilities of the future. There are variables in play, however, that can change what is seen from psychic to psychic. However, not every person in a sun sign is going through the exact same situations at the same time. Individual readings are the absolute best you can get.

Want to start but don't know what to do? The best thing is to go watch tarot readers on YouTube. See how they shuffle their cards, how they lay their spread out, the clarifying they do, how they group their cards and make connections. Watch what they do and focus a little less on what they say. You will find that everyone does them a little differently. While not critical, if you want to be a really good tarot reader, especially for others, you will have to dive into Astrology more as the two are very interconnected.

Do you have any friends who would be open to you reading for them? For free, mind you. You need to practice and have a fundamental understanding before you ever think of reading for money. If you don't have anyone in your circle, I suggest at least reading your own. It helps to get your mind working in a certain way.

I found in the beginning I needed to be careful tuning into one idea too strongly. Once you are an experienced reader, then sure, you will be able to get to that level. But you could in tune in a reading something is specific to their career versus their personal life simply because you know that person, instead of keeping it at a high level and seeing where it resonates. If that happens, look back and say, okay where did I screw up? Sometimes you find your friends haven't told you things that the cards then illustrate, and you go, oh. Until that point in time that you feel confident in reading and your readings verifying what the situations are, stay broader.

If you are wondering how you know when to stop the shuffle and when to start laying down cards. It's simple, listen to the voice in your head. Did you hear something say stop? Or maybe you did, but the cards got clunky at the end, and you heard, no, do one more? Whatever it is, whether you feel it is the moment, you hear something that says to stop, you go with that. If a card flies out while you are shuffling, don't put it back in, put it aside. That card had a specific message that needed to get across. After you do it enough, you will find that some cards repeatedly show up for you over a short period of time. It kind of feels like a stalker card. They will tell you the good, but they sure don't hold back on the bad either. There have been a few times where I pulled my cards and then just got up and walked away.

Some people let the reader touch their cards if they are physically present, Others don't want you to touch their cards at all. It doesn't really matter either way. A good intuitive doesn't need you present to do a reading. Make sure after you are done with a reading you clear the energy off your cards. If you find after a long time of using a deck and it seems to have gone sideways on you, burn the deck and get a new one.

CHAPTER 16

ALIENS VS GODS
AND RELIGION

I intentionally led you down this path of extraterrestrial life history and how it weaves into all the things I have noted previously. I did that because although it was woven through my journey and popped up very quickly before I did my Akashic Record reading in the beginning, the truth is I wanted to paint an overall picture for you of what I discovered.

I have found a variety of people to be in various states of awake. Some have all the info. Some have most. Some chose to find their life purpose during their Awakening, but never completely went down the full path of it, and are only partially awake on knowledge because they are still operating under the bulk of their existing belief systems, which is a fundamentally part of the problem.

They actually got caught in a trap in their Awakening by becoming solely focused on what they believed their purpose to be, and not fully realizing the bigger picture. We need everyone to complete it. Come to acceptance with it, sit in the full knowledge of it. Purge the horrors and trauma from their consciousness and heal.

I've found a large group of people that completely buy in to the extraterrestrial concept of advanced beings greater than ourselves and the history of the Earth not being depicted accurately, but the rest of the consciousness stuff, past lives, spirits and all that, is where they can't go. Most of these people are not religious, because they have found that aliens and religion under monotheistic religions cannot simultaneously exist. Among, of course, their personal views and experiences they have had with religion. Thus I wanted those people to read my journey first in that area, in order to then tie in what they may already know or believe at the end.

There are others that can get behind the spirit and consciousness discussion much easier than the aliens, so for those people, it's easier to bring them down the path they already have a comfort level with yet portraying it in a slightly different way than maybe it has been previously delivered. At that point, then we can tie in the aliens and blow your mind. Because, my mind was blown.

You have been lied to. Deceived, intentionally, for thousands of years by your governments and your religious leaders. They think you aren't capable of handling the truth. They also realize the truth coming to light is a problem. Because it means that everything they have been spouting off at you as the way, is in fact, not accurate. Imagine for a moment a spaceship with some humanoid people drop out of the sky one day here and walk off a ship and tell us something that illustrates why you shouldn't be worshipping any gods or religions because extraterrestrial life has been interchanging on Earth for millions of years. How does the Pope reconcile that for his worshippers? He can't really. How do the governments reconcile their party lines that align with religion now? Problem there. How do governments save face to the public when the aliens tell everyone that the government knew and has been working with them for decades? They can't.

I have talked about Starseeds being light-based consciousness that originated from another star system and planet(s) that are currently on Earth, helping to raise the vibrational frequency of humans at this time. Once you have leaned into that, you are smack in the middle of the alien debate. And you realize you inevitably are going to be drawn into the alien discussion currently on Earth. That was one of the interesting developments in this process, weaving the metaphysical plane in with the human plane to make it more tangible. Once you lean into the alien concept, you realize you have a conflict with the religion concept as how it has previously been presented. In fact, when you do your research, what you find is that there are elements of all religions that actually have art and inferences to aliens or alien technology through art. All pointing the finger that our primary history is not just the last 13,000 years. In fact, there is much more to the story. But you still have questions. These gods mentioned, how can they not be part of the story? Oh, they are.

So who were these Gods in all these religions? God in the Bible? The fallen angels? The Greek gods? The Norse gods? The Annunaki? Shiva?

Simply different races of humanoids with advanced knowledge and psychic capabilities from another planet. The Greek Gods if you step back and analyze it was a larger human that simply has access to psychic abilities. Poseidon was able to manipulate water. Zeus could manipulate electrical currents. The Goddess Athena, telepathic, could remote view, manipulate energy like Zeus, clairvoyant and clairaudient. You can't beat someone like that in war. Not sure where Shiva was from, but definitely an extraterrestrial taking advantage of inferior intelligent beings. The

Egyptians otherwise known as the Annunaki? Extraterrestrials from another planet. Some call their planet Nibiru, some call it Planet X. Some believe it is in an elliptical loop every 13,000 years it comes into our solar system, shoots around our sun ,and goes back out. That the energetic pull from this planet causes end-of-the-world type catastrophes to occur.

The Annunaki story is one of the most complicated and convoluted ones I had to work through. I kept getting stuck in loops of disinformation, and it was becoming difficult to sort through what was what. There is a lot of information out there and a lot of people who give a decent synopsis of them. Barbara Marciniak does a great job covering the Annunaki as well as Sonny Ramirez with his book *Annunaki: Gods of Earth and Nibiru*

In short, the Annunaki came to Earth to mine for gold because their planet was dying, and they needed gold to save it. They weren't here to build the pyramids. That was just the center of the Earth, essentially from an energetic perspective, as well as being a beautiful place at the time. They had advanced technology they used, and they brought a human slave race with them to mine the gold. At one point, one of the Annunaki brothers decided he wanted to rule. This where Egyptian history starts to shift, and you see where there are breaks in what happens next. The main guy Enki comes back and decides to blow everything up. This seems to be what caused the Great Flood.

Before my journey, this was my belief system. I was a former Catholic that had dropped my religion two decades prior. There were things along the way I had naturally questioned. Things just didn't make sense to me. The whole Jesus conception was extremely difficult for me because my stepfather was an OB /GYN, and my mother was a nurse. So conception was scientific and proven. The only reply anyone would ever say is, it was divine intervention. Well WTF does that mean when it comes to science? Is science wrong? If Jesus was born on Earth, then where did he go for thirty years? Why was there no record of him during Roman times until he was propped up in the Bible? My original theory in my youth was that he either was in prison for a big chunk of it and had one of those enlightenment in prison moments or he traveled to Asia and was steeped in Eastern Religious teachings for years and then came back. But if he did exist, and then you have questions about the tomb and where did his body go? Well, a little telekinesis and his extraterrestrial family taking his body away to help perpetuate a story. I can get behind that. Even in the New Age, no one really wants to go there on the Jesus topic because they associate him as an ascended master, but I think it's a good idea.

Why did God tell a guy to sacrifice his kid? That seems pretty extreme. If a God or another entity told me to sacrifice my child, I would tell them to fuck right off. No question. Should you really have to obey your parents? What if they are bad people and abuse you or are just not competent to be a parent due to drug use? That obey thing seems a bit askew on if they are good or bad people, and I did not like the word obey. It made me feel like I was a dog. SIT. STAY. DO THIS NOT THAT. What is this nonsense with menstrual periods? I was raised where I learned about sex in a completely non-emotional way. It was biology, plain and simple. I watched videos on female reproductive stuff growing up in my parents' offices at an early age. So to say it was possible for someone to get pregnant "magically," just was a stretch in my mind. There was the shame I felt in being a woman reading the Bible or when it was read to me. Women were like dogs and should be treated as such. The Koran is no different with its teachings on women. You want to marry a woman, and she sucks so bad that not only do you have to give her away, you have to give more of your shit away to get rid of her, and be grateful for it? Does that even make logical sense? No. That's some archaic thinking right there.

Something happened that started the full shift in my belief structure at 19. I remember one day actually saying out loud to myself, "I am done with this." I just can't get behind religion and the rules. After doing so, I immediately felt like a weight had been lifted off my shoulders. I no longer felt like a bad person. I also very much felt, if there is a hell then these are my people cause I can't get behind the religious people. Like the world was a lighter place all of a sudden. I had decided, if hell was where I was going to go because I wasn't going to submit into a subservient system with ideas I just could not get behind, then I was going to be in hell with a lot of good people, and that was something I could get behind.

The idea that someone can violate another human being, go to confession, and they get to go to heaven, but a homosexual is damned regardless of how moral and ethical they were as a human being in every other aspect of their life, I couldn't get behind that. To see the hypocrites that sat in church to assure their ticket to heaven, yet not living a path of righteousness, they get to go. But the Africans who don't know about Christianity, oh those poor people are fucked. Does that seem right to you? It certainly does not seem logical.

Even as a teenager, I would go to my friend's churches. I was interested in the experience. How was it different from mine? What did I like, not like? How did it make me feel? I continued this kind of curiosity in discussions with people as I grew as an adult. I had discovered early on, there were running themes in all religions really. So what were those themes?

Religion is rooted in stories. Previous stories were handed down like the telephone game and then selected by a certain group of special people. So you have to be careful not to lean into a story word for word, and instead, look for what the story is saying. Does that story corroborate in another story? What are the differences? What are the things in the story that seem ... off? I remember stumping my mother on Bible stories all the time as a kid. Walking away with an answer that didn't quite satisfy my question. As an adult, I am a bit horrified thinking of my son learning about slaughtering firstborn children in God's name, as noted in the Bible. In fact, the Bible is a collection of stories written by people after Jesus was born. The Gospel wasn't written by Matthew, Mark, Luke, and John, or even close to the time they lived.

"It has served us well this myth of Christ. What profit has not that fable of Christ brought us," said, Pope Leo X

Trauma incurred during childhood or trauma incurred as an adult are both awful. But I'm going to focus on trauma of the child. The root of these problems is solely in the realm of raising a child, and the negative forces at play know this. If you can corrupt a child, then you can gain control over them and propagate that individual into fear-based, shame-based, lack of self-worth energy that is used to fuel negative entity agendas. Because the truth is, a child that does not incur abuse (which includes neglect, among other things), grows up to be an adult who does not abuse others nor is violent.

This is proven in psychology that the root of all psychosis stems from childhood experiences. That trauma could have been incurred by a parent, a sibling, family member, or any individual in a position of power and authority that has access to a child. To complicate matters in this situation is when a child is abused by a family member or person the parent trusted, and as a result, when the trauma is revealed to them, they don't want to believe it because believing it means they have to own their role in it. Whether it was simply trusting the individual in question or the refusal to believe that the individual would have hurt their child. Complicating it further is when a child is abused, but another child wasn't. In that scenario, there is a default of, well, it didn't happen to me therefore, it didn't happen to you. Then you have people who just don't want to believe. There is already so much shame wrapped up in the victim of abuse.

Growing up in the Catholic Church, I was an Altar girl but never had an experience with a priest that was sexual, but that does not mean I don't believe every single person who has claimed they were abused at the hands of a church member. I do believe them. I totally see how it can happen and not even be detected. The three safest places for a child have predominantly been their home, a church, and school. When those areas are corrupted, then it makes it very difficult to feel safe as a child.

The Catholic Church is by far the biggest organized corrupter of children by men in a position of power and authority. What is worse is we are now starting to hear stories of Nuns also being sexually abused in horrific ways. Lucetta Scaraffia has been spearheading the #NunsToo movement to bring light to the sexual and physical abuse that has been done to nuns in an effort to stop it. As a nun, when you commit to the church, this isn't a paid position. God and The Church will take care of you, so there is no need for you to have any money. So if you have no money, then you can't get out of your situation. Nice trap, isn't it?

The Church has firmly rooted themselves against science in biology in this area by proclaiming that priests and nuns cannot marry nor are they supposed to engage in ANY sexual activity. Ask any man if they can go a week straight without touching themselves, and you will be laughed at. So what happens is a priest has to fight against how the body is designed and repress these emotions or feelings that they would otherwise be able to express in a normal relationship. When that happens they seek out a way to release the pressure that has been building. They do so by targeting individuals that they are able to have power over. Then they become a repeat offender because they enjoy it.

The body was designed to procreate and to enjoy sexual energy. It isn't something you can suppress simply because you said a vow to God. And now the Church has boxed themselves into a corner. Because they are not taking full ownership of the atrocities, their clergy have committed. They refuse to in the face of it being exposed. Maybe they reassign someone, forced him into retirement, and all they do is say an Our Father for those poor souls who were hurt. They don't need a prayer. They need you to completely change your traditions and habits because it doesn't functionally work, and we are starting to expose all of it. Where they get themselves into a further problem is, if you start changing a fundamental layer of fabric of the Church by allowing clergy to get married, give up the vow of chastity, you start to unravel the very foundation that props them up. Remember, in religion, you can't just start changing the rules, because if you start changing the rules, then people think the rules can be changed, and if they can be changed, then they want other rules to start being changed. Personally, I wish all religion was dead. It is a virus that infects the human mind.

I had been taught the same scientific stuff everyone had been taught growing up about the history of the Earth, how old it was, how it started, evolution of man. But I didn't buy it. Something just seemed off to me. Like, they were really reaching for some things, and some other things just didn't make sense. I mean, the Earth is 4.6 Billion years old, and the oldest human life found is approximately 300,000 years old, but really, our roots only go back about 13,000 years? Yet it took billions of years for the Earth to become habitable in the first place? I wasn't buying it but would wait until someone came up with some other plausible theory.

I had grown up always thinking it would be cool if there was extra-terrestrial life. But I never was around a lot of those kinds of discussion topics. Devout religious people don't discuss extraterrestrials, the concept that there is advanced life outside of us, or anything that interferes with the sovereign God concept. Over the years, as an adult and more and more stories of UFO crashes, sightings, abductions occurred, I bought in to the theory that there was definitely advanced life like us in the universe. I just didn't think I would ever see it in this lifetime since the idea was that we would have to find it first. We couldn't even get past the moon. It was the psychic content that shoved me down the rabbit hole. It was the spiritual and alien stuff that pulled it all together and showed me the big picture.

By the time I eventually came to my Awakening two decades later, I was already halfway there. I believed in something greater. I just didn't know what exactly. My political views had changed based on how my views on humanity changed based on the experiences I had with others.

An easy thing to do, look into ancient stories from indigenous people. Look at the pictures and look to see if maybe the objects in the picture look like aliens, or maybe a human in a spacesuit or a spacecraft. You will find even in the Bible if you change "angels" and the "voices from the sky" out to be "extraterrestrials," you get a different picture.

To bring all this conceptual talk back around into the human plane of reality we have been operating in and how can we make any of this more tangible. We lead into the conspiracy theory section. I knew when the alien discussion first came up in this path that it was going to lead me right into conspiracy theories. What I did not expect it to do, is lead me into ALL the conspiracy theories by showing how they connect.

CHAPTER 17

CONSPIRACY THEORIES ... OR ARE THEY?

I never wanted to write anything about conspiracy theories. But failing to do so defeats the purpose of this book. The truth is conspiracy theories are riddled throughout spirituality discussions. Before I deep dive into this section, I'm going to start out with the conspiracy theory traps.

CONSPIRACY THEORIES TRAP 1

Thinking all conspiracy theories are true because some are. Not all conspiracy theories are true at all. In fact, I would venture to say that most conspiracy theories as they are known today are a combination of truths and misinformation. As a result, you need to be careful going headfirst into all conspiracy theories and taking them for the gospel as they are presented. It is okay to believe part of a conspiracy theory but not all of it because some you can't discredit. It's also okay not to believe every conspiracy theory out there, which leads me into Trap #2.

TRAP 2

QAnon & Anonymous. Let me start by saying quite simply. What The Fuck. QAnon happens to be one of the worst of the traps in this entire process. In fact, I've been extremely disappointed in the amount of my spiritual community that stepped right into this trap and bit down hard. QAnon slowly came into being around 2017. For me, there was a weirdness about that, though, when I started hearing it gained traction because I could have sworn I had been hearing about Anonymous for at least a decade in random things here and there.

Anonymous is an organization that started as a bunch of hackers specifically going after governments, institutions, and agencies. Many individuals that operate in groups for cyber ops are devoted to leftist-libertarian ideals of personal freedom and opposed to the consolidation of corporate and government power. The basic idea was exposing confidential information that specifically showed atrocities and underhanded government or corporate operations against groups of civilians.

QAnon, on the other hand, is a far-right conspiracy group started in 2017 off a site called 4Chan alleging that a group of high-ranking government officials and Hollywood elites who are Satan-worshipping pedophiles that are running a global child sex-trafficking ring and that former President #45 is secretly fighting to expose the cabal.

It took some digging on this and reading the actual breakdown of the difference between the two written by Anonymous and the outing/trashing of Q as a false flag type of conspiracy group, to make sense of this. The irony of the Q followers is just like in the movie *Now You See Me 2*, where the character Atlas is secretly getting messages from a source called The Eye awaiting their next magician assignment of a new high-profile target to take down. Except it ends up being revealed that the person communicating as The Eye isn't The Eye at all, and it was a trap by the very guy that was setting them up for the fall all along. Designed to lure this group of magicians into a situation as payback for what they did to the family in Now You See Me. It was a combination of misdirection (Trust The Plan) feeding into the magician's desire to be part of this group called The Eye that landed them in this trap. In the end, The Real Eye is revealed and even shown how they were assisting the magicians in getting out of the trap they landed in with The Fake Eye. That's basically what has happened to Q followers. Only they don't even realize they took the bait and bit down hard and never used discernment in any form.

Let's break it down. Government officials and Hollywood elites who are involved in child sex trafficking rings who drink the blood of babies for aging reduction properties and who are part of the plan for the New World Order. First of all, the misdirection is to make them look away at the hard truth on pedophilia and sex trafficking by making them focus on something that isn't close to home. A way to push the blame for these items elsewhere. The reality is pedophilia and sex trafficking are much closer to home than that and pervasive everywhere. Let's start with say, the Catholic Church, The Boy Scouts of America, youth sports coaches (Larry Nassar, Jerry Sandusky ring a bell). Have we conveniently forgotten about those? Why doesn't Q actively direct the focus and attention on those groups?

Additionally, Q getting you riled up about a secret society that may or may not be doing these things, is getting you to deflect your attention off what you should be doing, which is rooting out the sexual abuse within your own circle of family and friends—healing your immediate group. Basically, pedophilia at its core is done by any person who is in a position of power or authority over a minor. It's a pretty broad concept which means that it isn't isolated to Hollywood or government officials. Weird shit happens all over the planet. I mean, there are people who dress up as animals and have sex. People who swear they are vampires. So the weird is out there. Is pedophilia happening by people in Hollywood and Government circles? Of course it is. But it is happening in almost every single family line in the world. If you dig into child sex abuse statistics, you find appalling numbers.

According to the National Association of Adult Survivors of Child Abuse, there are more than forty-two million survivors of child abuse in the United States alone. One in three girls are abused before the age of eighteen. One in five boys are abused before the age of eighteen. One in five children are solicited on the internet before the age of eighteen. Twenty percent of reported cases are to children under the age of eight. At least 30% of sexual abuse is never reported. Almost 70% of all sexual assaults occur to children under the age of seventeen.

Now sit with this statistic for a minute. 90% of all child sexual abuse victims KNOW their abuser in some way.

Individuals with a developmental delay or disability have a 90% chance they will be assaulted sometime in their life. There are currently half a million registered sex offenders in the United States. And if that doesn't horrify you, then chew on the idea that a typical pedophile will commit over one hundred sexual crimes in their lifetime.

When you look at sex trafficking just in the United States alone, you find out that most children who are trafficked are homeless, ran away, or were kicked out of their homes for being LGBTQ. If you sat in a room with thirty people, then basically, there are ten people in that room that are victims of child sexual abuse. And some of the people in the room are sexual predators. If you have a family gathering of eighteen people for Christmas, that means that six people in the room were abused (and at least one are predators). The reality being, most likely by another family member or a friend of the family in some capacity.

When we look at the section on Healing, we have to realize the trauma is much closer to home than we are comfortable with. If you weren't abused, then someone you love was, and if you don't know, then it is a dark family secret no one talks about. People will use the idea that their sister couldn't have been abused by the favorite uncle, because they weren't abused by the uncle, but that doesn't mean their sister wasn't abused. The idea you have to face the demons in your own inner circle is difficult for most people to accept, which is why it is easier to say—oh look, people in Hollywood we have no interaction with, they are the pedophile group.

This is the reason I don't completely buy into the theory that Earth is just a school for learning, and we all just swap roles and play a part in everyone's growth. Sit in the headspace and ask yourself if you willingly would accept the role to be a sexual predator? When you sit in the headspace of agreeing to be a victim of abuse, your mind directs to, why would I do that? Well, if you buy into the ideology of Starseeds and that we are here to be the breaker of chains and generational curses, that part makes sense. To not turn around and become predators and to eventually stop the repeated patterns. Additionally, if you believe there is an agenda of higher dimensional beings or aliens that have some form of control over humans or are feeding off human energy, then the tentacles of fear, shame, guilt, trauma that are inflicted upon a human, especially a child, makes a lot of sense. When children are abused, it affects them for the rest of their life in many different capacities.

Next point, #45 is/was secretly going to expose all sorts of corrupt officials and elites, and a massive amount of sealed indictments have been issued or will be any day to bring down the Deep State. So did he do that? Nope. Let's add in the fact that he also has been accused by twenty-six women of sexual assault over the years, and he is directly linked to Jeffrey Epstein. Additionally, for anyone paying attention, #45 has never done anything that doesn't serve his own self-interest. So to believe he is doing anything for the good of the people is ludicrous.

How have we been lied to and deceived by our leaders? Well, the Roman Catholic Church has about five miles of historical documentation in their vaults. They are a sovereign state in the middle of a country. Surrounded by a moat.

The Roman Empire started in approximately 27 BC. The Roman Catholic Church was formed approximately 30 AD supposedly to align with the teachings of Christ. Their conquering controlled most of Europe, the entire Mediterranean including the northern coast of Africa, parts of the Middle East and Asia. Now to put that in practical terms, what they conquered and confiscated covered the territories of ancient civilizations of Mesopotamia, Indus Valley, Ancient Egypt, Ancient Greece, and Persia. Five of the ten oldest civilizations, not including themselves in that list. The others are the Incan, Mayan, Aztec, and Chinese civilizations. Documented history that goes back to at least 3,000 BC … that we know of. Yet, we also know that humans have been on Earth for at least 300,000 years due to skeletons found in Morocco and ice age paintings in caves in France. That is quite the gap. Add the gap in the DNA sequence that scientists can't figure out how we made the leap from homo erectus, nor can they truly link us to apes as a hybrid species.

The types of human remains found are classified as Neanderthals, Homo neanderthalensis, Denisovans, Homo erectus, and Homo rhodesiensis. Several short, small-brained species: Homo naledi, Homo luzonensis, Homo floresiensis, and the Red Deer Cave People in China. By 10,000 years ago, they were extinct with no known environmental catastrophe. The extinctions' timing points to the possibility of a tide of a new species, evolving 260,000-350,000 years ago: Homo sapiens.

Back to the Catholic Church, the Vatican Archives have been estimated to contain 8 kilometers (5 mi) of shelving. They allegedly contain all the pope's letters and include the oldest written known version of the Bible. But we haven't had that many popes to fill 8 kilometers of space. The archives are a private library that no one has access to. So what is in their vaults? What is in there that they don't want the public en masse to know about?

THE CABAL/ILLUMINATI

The Cabal or Illuminati are a group of old wealthy bloodlines going back many centuries who are really pulling the strings on a global stage and are behind all major events and decisions in the world. On the surface, this seems like a ludicrous idea. I certainly thought it was. But the more I dug into it, the more I started to realize it isn't as crazy as it sounds. I think most of us can get behind the generalization that the government doesn't have our best interest at the forefront, and they aren't to be trusted. They have lied and deceived the American public about a million things. And really all governments throughout history across the glove have. It doesn't matter what side of the table you are on in politics. The overwhelming majority of them are not looking out for the people or passing bills that are for the good of the collective. I struggled with this idea for a while, until I did a deeper dive into politics on the world stage and how the media is inherently owned by six corporations and how the food supply is controlled, regulated, and distributed, in conjunction with how the pharmaceutical companies and the healthcare industry is all managed. Add in the central banking system that is controlled by a single family (Rothschild) of all countries' banking systems except three, and this concept became hard to shrug off. I started to get more behind that possibility of a Cabal type of secret government. But then it morphed into child sex trafficking and drinking the blood of babies, and #45 is the savior. At this point, it was a bridge too far, and I had to step back and look at it again. Remember that deflection and discernment are keys in all of this.

The basis of why I am even writing this book is to get people to look inside themselves. To see things in a different light and one in which they understand everything from their choices in the human plane, the spiritual plane, and the steps they need to take to break out of the system, heal themselves and elevate and grow their consciousness so we can all stop repeating these awful patterns the human race likes to play out. It is much easier to yell into the void about a group of people you don't actually know about doing some heinous thing than it is to focus your attention on the abuses within your own immediate sphere of influence. Thereby perpetuating a lack of growth and healing in a situation you have influence on. This keeps you suppressed in your evolution. All the while, convincing you that you are a truther and exposing the lies to the masses.

I am not saying that there aren't groups of people doing some really awful and off-the-wall shit out there, because I think the internet has already proven that there is. But be careful what you go headfirst into believing and what the possible motivations behind the ones pushing the theories might be.

Which leads into the topic of a False Flag. A false flag scenario is one where an act is committed with the intent of pinning it on the opposite party, but the actual source of the false flag is disguised. It's textbook misdirection maneuvers. For example, you could take a situation about mass shootings, and one side will say this is orchestrated by the Democrats to try and take away your gun rights. Or, it could be orchestrated by Republicans because gun sales go up after mass shootings. There are different lenses to view situations through.

CONNECTING THE OLD AND THE NEW, A TRIP DOWN THE LAST 100 YEARS.

Let's run down some basic timelines and also some of the most common conspiracy theories as a way to illustrate where we have been led astray and why we can't trust our government leaders, religious leaders, and to some degree, even historians.

LATE 1800S TO MID-1900S
+ John Rockefeller makes his millions in oil
+ JP Morgan makes his millions in American finance
+ 1888 George Eastman founds Eastman Kodak
+ 1887 Tesla creates the alternating conduction motor, essentially the same motor that could power the world as in Ayn Rand's Atlas Shrugged. Side note: Tesla worked at the Edison company before branching out on his own.
+ 1891 Tesla patents the Tesla Coil, which is the first step to wireless electricity and communications. He also is responsible for X-ray technology and radio communications devices. Due to Tesla's research, the US was one of the first countries to deploy wireless radio communications in our military exercises in WW1.
+ 1934 Orson Welles gives his fictional live broadcast on War of the Worlds
+ 1939 Hitler sends military units to Antarctica
+ 1943 Nikolas Tesla mysteriously dies, most of his research is seized by the US Government
+ 1945 The US drops the Atom bomb

+ 1945 WWII ends, Hitler escapes to Argentina—watch the documentary Hunting Hitler to see where they proved he did not die in the bunker. Also note that Hitler was highly into the occult as well as investigations into Antarctica. Why was that?

+ 1945 (to 1959) Operation Paperclip was a secret program of the Joint Intelligence Objectives in which more than 1,600 German scientists, engineers, and technicians, such as Wernher von Braun and his team, were taken from Germany to America for US government employment. Many were former leaders of the Nazi party. The primary purpose for Operation Paperclip was US military advantage in the Soviet–American Cold War and the Space Race. The reason we made it into space and onto the moon—Wernher von Braun. In fact, when you look into him further, you see that he also leaned into metaphysical concepts and was an intuitive as well, and his goal was to make it to Mars. He was another one of those people that literally changed the landscape of humans with his ingenuity and knowledge that seemed ahead of his time.

+ June 21, 1947, Maury Island WA UFO Sighting

+ July 8, 1947, Roswell NM UFO Incident

+ September 18, 1947, CIA, USAF, and Department of Defense formed—3 months after Roswell.

+ 1947 Operation High Jump—Admiral Richard Byrd led 4,000 military troops from the US, Britain, and Australia in an invasion of Antarctica, and at least one follow-up expedition.

+ 1952 NSA founded.

+ 1952 Project Blue Book was a series of studies of UFOs conducted by the US Air Force. Project Blue Book had two goals: To determine if UFOs were a threat to national security, and to scientifically analyze UFO-related data.

+ 1955/6 Operation Deep freeze military expeditions to Antarctica
+ 1958 NASA founded
+ 1960 Brookings Report is released and was commissioned by NASA to determine "The implications of a discovery of extraterrestrial life," which examines the potential implications of such a discovery on public attitudes and values. It considers possible public reactions to possible scenarios for the discovery of extraterrestrial life, stressing a need for further research in this area. It recommended continuing studies to determine the likely social impact of such a discovery and its effects on public attitudes, including studying the question of how leadership should handle information about such a discovery and under what circumstances leaders might or might not find it advisable to withhold such information from the public. They determined, the public was not capable of being alerted to the existence of advanced extraterrestrial life. One of the main reasons? Because it blows the doors open on the monotheistic religions in the world that had a stronghold in billions of people's lives.
+ 1961 Antarctic Treaty System was executed which currently has 54 parties.
+ 1961 first US man in space Alan Shepherd
+ 1962 First supercomputer unveiled (15 years after Roswell)
+ 1962 first US man in orbit John Glenn
+ 1963 JFK Assassinated—important as in research you find that JFK was going to expose top-secret alien information.
+ 1955–75 Vietnam War where various servicemen, including high-ranking officials, have now come forward with unexplained occurrences and UFO sightings during the war. Does that war not seem odd to you? 58,000 US servicemen died, two million North and South Vietnamese civilians died. It is an area of 331,000 sq

miles or approximately twice the size of Florida, and after twenty years, we failed. Seems odd don't you think? Not when you start reading about former US military men mentioning spacecraft that attacked them when the Viet Cong didn't even have helicopters. Stories of being shot at, shooting back, but when investigating, there is nothing there and doesn't look like there was. It was like we were fighting an invisible army.

+ 1969 first man on the moon Neil Armstrong
+ 1973 first cell phone

The presidents on record stating they believe in the existence of advanced extraterrestrial life: Eisenhower, Nixon, JFK, Carter, Reagan, Clinton, Obama. One could consider #45's odd declaration in 2016, a few months after he took office, that we would create a military branch called Space Force. Why is that necessary?

Paul Hellyer, the former Canadian Minister of National Defense, is on record saying the US has been working with advanced extraterrestrials and there are up to twelve known different types of ET's inhabiting the planet. Nick Pope worked for the British Military of Defense in investigating UFO phenomena. Even a high-ranking former Israeli Space official just came out that there is a Galactic Confederation that has been working with the US for decades and told #45 to keep it quiet. There are loads of service- men and women who have stories. There are sightings all over the world. With the advent of social media, people are sharing videos and pictures of unexplained UFO phenomenon. This means we are no longer as reliant on the media to provide us with what they want us to consume.

When you run down that list and realize that the explosion of the human race with technology came with the advancements of Tesla and then the Roswell incident and that we made progress that was leaps above all the centuries before, you realize the governments have been lying through their teeth on this topic.

At this point, we can pretty much all agree ETs have been on Earth for a millennium and are currently. Which then leads you to ask, why are they leaving us alone? Sure we could counter that with the crop circles and livestock mutilations and abductions that have happened. But let's be realistic. They have better technology, but they haven't really used it on it like they could. Why? It certainly indicates a lack of fear with them living in tandem with us. And what does that indicate? Is it an inferiority thing? Or are they controlling us somehow? I will say, at this point, our governments are all acting like the emperor with no clothes. They can keep saying there are no aliens, but everyone knows the emperor has no clothes on because we see it with our own eyes. So if one of our governments all of a sudden trots out some alien crew and says we are in an alliance, you should have an immediate red flag pop up. That would be called a false flag.

In your research, you will find all sorts of wild things out there. Again, use your own discernment to determine how something does or does not resonate with you. I am going to break some of them down for you in a way that will allow you to search out on your own.

THE MOON

This one blew my mind when I first read about it, and then I watched the *Ancient Aliens* episode on it, and they break it all down for you. I highly suggest you go watch that episode because you will want to deny this one. The oddities of the moon: it doesn't spin/rotate. It rotates in orbit around the Earth in what is called synchronous rotation. Now they say that it actually does orbit the Earth once every 27.322 days, while it also takes approximately twenty-seven days for it to rotate once on its axis. But this is still odd. Moons naturally get a pull from the planets they orbit due to the energy of the planet and its electromagnetic fields, and they do so at a faster pace. Because the moon is in this synchronous rotation, we only see one side of it. That is why it was a really big deal that the Chinese sent a craft and landed on the dark side of the moon on January 3, 2019, because no one had been to the dark side of the moon, and because we can't see it from the vantage point of Earth. No Earthlings have seen it from a telescope either.

Now the theory is that the moon is not actually a moon but instead a spaceship or satellite of sorts. Here is why. The mathematical dimensions of where the moon is placed in orbit with Earth is too mathematically precise.

When the Apollo 11 mission left the moon and subsequent missions, they left seismology equipment behind. When the crew detached the Lunar Module and sent it crashing back to the surface, when it hit, the seismometers not too far away recorded what sounded like a giant bell ringing under the surface of the moon. And it rang for almost an hour. Other instances from NASA between 1972 to 1977 recorded similar recordings, one lasting as long as three hours recorded to about twenty to twenty-five miles below the surface. Now in order for something to reverberate sound in that manner, it means it has to have a hollow chamber in order for the sound to resonate. Which means, the moon has a hollow core.

Additionally, NASA cut the feed for several minutes while they were up there. Why? When the Apollo 11 astronauts came back to Earth and had their press conference, why were they not excited or overwhelmed? They looked like they were in shock about something.

The chemical composition of the moon's surface doesn't make sense. The first is the crater impact. When you look at all the craters on the moon, none of them make a deep impact like we would expect on Earth if something like that hit our surface. In fact, there are really wide craters that are not very deep. The chemical breakdown of the moon's surface are three components—basalt, titanium, and magnesium and then meteorite remnants. These components, according to the geologist on Ancient Aliens, are the ingredients that if you were to make some sort of hollowed-out spaceship from a planet like structure to deal with impacts, weather, and radioactive solar energy exposure since the moon does not have an ionosphere.

The other oddity is there are some indigenous tribes whose stories tell of a time before the moon was in the sky. Not to mention, all the current theories the scientists have don't hold water in most people's view. Because they can't come up with a valid scientific explanation, they theorize the moon is a creation of two spheres that collided. That does not resonate with me. If you took two round objects and smashed them together, they don't magically form a new round object.

Why have we not been back to the moon since the 70s? It doesn't add up. You may be saying, but wait, we have the tides in the ocean that the moon has a direct impact on us. That is because the moon reflects the light and energy of the sun back to Earth. So the more exposure to the full surface of the moon, the more impact back to Earth during what we see is a full moon. If you aren't aware, the reason we see the moon in phases is that the Earth blocks the moon in its rotation around the sun, and thus, the moon gets exposed to different amounts of solar energy in that path that it redirects. It's still okay to bathe your crystals in the moonlight. It's just a calmer solar energy.

Some people believe the moon landing was faked, and Stanley Kubrick filmed it. But I don't subscribe to that theory. I think Kubrick might have been involved in promotional materials and effects, but we went to the moon.

MARS AND THE PLANET MALDEK

To understand that the Earth is four billion years old and is considered a young planet and that there are more advanced beings out there, then you start seeing information about Mars and Maldek. If you look at the asteroid belt, it is a perfect alignment to where a planet would be, if there could be one. And why are the asteroids in a stasis-type orbit? The destruction of Maldek was an attempt at fighting against Mars contingents and in the process, it backfired, and they essentially blew themselves up. The impact was so destructive it fried Mars, and the asteroids in the asteroid belt are remnants of the planet.

The Mars Rover that NASA dropped up there that has been taking pictures revealed a lot of peculiarities. The oddities that appear to mirror ancient Egyptian items. Max Spiers, in an interview before his suspicious death, said he remembered living on Mars, and before he evacuated, he strung a bunch of activation codes around his spine to make sure he would wake up and remember certain things at certain points in time. When Maldek blew, many Mars evacuees came to Earth, and the souls that fragmented from the explosion ended up coming to Earth to wait for a new life incarnation. When you look at Mars and read what the scientists are now starting to understand about Mars is that it could have sustained life at some point, and with some terraforming, it probably could, in pockets, hold life in the future. It would be ironic if we left Mars to come to Earth to eventually go back to Mars. If you want to read how the Annunaki came to Earth, then read up on Corey Goode's experiences. He links in Antarctica as well and the thirteen bloodlines (Illuminati). I suggest reading this stuff once you get a grip on Earth first. Corey Goode's stuff is for when you are ready to really level up.

THE ARK OF THE COVENANT

Ever wonder what is actually in the Ark of the Covenant? This one always intrigued me as a child in Bible study. What was really in the Ark of the Covenant, and why is it missing? The Bible said it contained the stone tablets of the 10 Commandments along with the manna machine Moses and his followers used while wandering the desert for forty years. However, another Ancient Alien episode covered this one as well. When you go back to the Bible and the description of the Ark of the Covenant, it was a solid wooden box covered in gold. You know what is fantastic about gold? It is one of the few metals that can absorb radiation exposure efficiently.

George Sasson, an engineer, and Rodney Dale wrote a book called The Manna Machine based upon a section of the Zohar called The Ancient of Days. It concludes that a machine had created green algae as food for human beings in biblical times. NASA even did a test with astronauts in space where they subsisted for thirty days only on green algae. Using the description of the machine, they reverse engineered it and noted that to make it work, the only things needed were water vapor and solar energy that they could get from the air and a small nuclear reactor. But if we look at history, nuclear technology wasn't in play at that time, was it? If you look at stories about the Ark of the Covenant being used to vanquish enemies, you realize the descriptions of the death incurred by the Ark of the Covenant are the same as radiation poisoning from exposure. Just like Chernobyl.

THE MATRIX

Are we in a holographic matrix-like some believe? Are we just in a reality game or show for other extraterrestrials? Well, one could say that if extraterrestrials possess significantly more advanced technology than ours and if the moon is a control ship, then I don't see a conflict as other terrestrials could effectively view things going on down here on Earth like changing a channel on the TV. Some believe this is all one big play I would say a play is simply a simplified and rigid version of a video game or a matrix. Some believe we are on a prison planet. Well to some degree, if you can't get off/out of it, you are in a prison of sorts. Some refer to it as a zoo. I would say a zoo and a prison have a lot in common as far as animals in cages.

MELTING OF NUCLEAR WEAPON ARSENALS

Another theory is that extraterrestrials in 1991 melted down all the nuclear weapon arsenals on the planet because it is the wrong kind of technology to use. It has ripple effects far beyond simply our planet. I believe there was a military official on record somewhere confirming this, but I don't have the reference for that so unclear how accurate that is. This concept seems hard to believe, but I also am a little surprised we haven't been threatening nukes with anyone in the last thirty years. Side note, the Soviet Union fell apart in 1991. With that said, it has been heavily reported there is UFO activity around our military bases, and clearly, ETs are interested in what we are doing. If they contain technology dealing with physics we can't even comprehend yet, then it isn't too far of a stretch to conceive they might be able to neutralize other technologies.

THE ILLUMINATI/CABAL/NEW WORLD ORDER

I know I touched on this a little in the QAnon part, but I want to go into it deeper separately because this is not a conspiracy theory that spawned from QAnon, it simply became one of the ones the believes all bought into. It is a very old theory and is extremely entangled in all facets of economic, religious, geopolitical, and socio-economic life. This stems from the thirteen bloodlines anointed by the Annunaki (Ancient Egyptians) to rule when they left the planet. Is it possible they once existed? Probably. Do I think they still exist? Possibly. When you step back and look at who is controlling the main functions on our planet, the list isn't that large.

The New World Order is in reference to UN Agenda 2030 agreed to by all countries in 2015. The UN Agenda outlines it as the idea that the world is not currently sustainable on its current course with humans and thus a plan to achieve the goal of getting the nations of the world back to a sustainable place. The conspiracy theorists frame this as the Cabal's Depopulation Agenda. Then they point to how much landmass we have, and the UN argument is garbage. Let me clarify that for you.

We currently are contaminating our air. We are changing the chemical structure of it by cutting down half the Amazon rainforest, which is our atmosphere's vacuum cleaner. Our soil for farming is about twenty years from not being usable to grow crops. We are poisoning the freshwater we use, including the oceans. The lack of potable water across the world in supply for people outside the United States and Europe is a serious issue. We aren't able to feed the people we have and provide opportunities for them to thrive. Around 40% of the world lives in poverty. Almost 700 million people live in extreme poverty.

The conspiracy theory indicates that there is a global government or Cabal plan to kill off a large portion of the population as the solution to this problem. This is where you queue the COVID -9 virus conversation. A virus that wipes out a large part of the population. Look, I don't know how it started. Maybe it was in a lab—maybe it wasn't. What I do know is it was eerily strange that all the countries in the world just … shut down. They didn't know how bad it really was when they shut down, but they all just did. Unless our governments knew more information than what they told us. Which is also possible. But when has the Earth ever collectively ground to a halt? For me, that was the weirdest part of all of this. Like the regular citizens weren't getting all the information.

One of the conflicts I came to in this whole topic, though was this: the spiritual community is all for the collective consciousness and raising one's vibration. They channel different star beings. Those beings are classified as if they are a unified front from a given planet. But how do we really know that? How do you really know who is on whose side? I once listened to a Barbara Marciniak trance channeling, and the subject said the Pleadians were a tricky bunch. Or maybe it was sneaky, either way, that made me go, "Wait, that's not what I want to hear." The group that rages against a single unified global government manages to easily buy into it for other star systems and us communicating with them though. Seems to be a conflict in thought there.

This topic is back of the neck hair raising once I realized it wasn't a joke, and lots of people have died or been threatened who became too vocal. I caution you to be careful how far down this rabbit hole you go.

9/11 WAS AN INSIDE JOB

I really dislike this conspiracy theory. Because I can't disprove it based on what has been found. When I first heard 9/11 was an inside job, I was defiant that no it certainly was not. That is such a horrific thought. Exactly. It is horrific. But there are things that don't add up. The day before 9/11 Defense Secretary Donald Rumsfeld revealed that $2.3 trillion was unaccounted for in his department. 9/11 happens, and we all forget. The buildings had extra insurance taken out weeks before. How the hell did building 7 fall? Kiss my ass with the passport of the hijacker in the airplane that was found at ground zero. Were the docs of where the money went for the defense department conveniently where the plane hit the pentagon? There is some discrepancy on the CGI part of this, but explosion experts have weighed in that the twin towers also were detonated. This one will have you irate by the time you are done looking into it.

THE RAPTURE/APOCALYPSE/ASCENSION

People have been talking about this topic for centuries. The Rapture is a reference to Revelations in the Bible where the Earth ends, Jesus returns, there are wars, and the antichrist. The Apocalypse means revelation, as in something is uncovered. Ascension is the belief in your spirit rising to a higher dimension. Now some people think we are in the end of times, or near it. Other predictions still have a few more centuries before it happens. Some people believe in an elliptical orbit with a Dark Sun that every 26,000 years, the orbit causes a massive physical occurrence on Earth.

Many believe there will be an ascension but more like in the vein of how Dolores Cannon described. She had outlined from her client regressions that Earth was designed as a seed planet. It was to be a library of sorts. A collection of plants and animals and climates operating in a peaceful neutral planet where knowledge of solar systems and life would be retained. Humans were designed by other ETs. As Earth goes through her evolution in consciousness, so do the humans that are aligned to it. But it requires a push in that evolution, which is where the Starseeds come in. They were the push to lift the collective consciousness simply by the energy frequency they carry in their consciousness.

As part of this, there will be a splitting off of the Earth's consciousness and will be more like an etheric Earth. If you were to look at the Earth from the moon and you see the atmosphere glow, the split would kind of look like the atmosphere moved out of the Earth into its own bubble. When this shift occurs, the humans that have elevated their frequency to the right level will then transition to the new Earth with that shift. People on New Earth will be happy and saying "We did it!" Meanwhile, people on Old Earth will be confused about what is happening. The ones on Old Earth will have to go through another round of an ascension cycle on a different planet when they die. When the shift happens, it will be immediate. The difference between the Rapture and the Ascension is that religious people believe only religious people are going. Whereas the ascension is about your own personal spiritual evolution and elevation that is occurring in tandem with billions of other people. You either vibrate high enough or you don't.

Will this happen? Who knows. Could it happen in this lifetime? Possibly. If you think it might, then you better start working on sorting out your own shit, aka your shadow work if you want to make that shift. We know the Earth has gone through catastrophic cycles in her history. It could be a combination of the spiritual and human plane.

ATLANTIS AND LEMURIA

One of my favorite topics! Plato was the first to write about Atlantis. While scholars dismiss the writing as a piece of fiction, it doesn't account for the fact that many people have memories of Atlantis or Lemuria.

Lemuria was a continent in the Pacific Ocean. It stretched from the Galápagos Islands to Hawaii over to French Polynesia down to Fiji over to Easter Island and back up to the Galápagos Islands. The beings that lived on Lemuria were highly spiritual and humanoid but not human. They were a peaceful people.

Atlantis was first thought to be a city, but then it was thought to be a civilization encompassing an entire continent. Many have tried to find

Atlantis, and there are a couple of possibilities. One is that Antarctica is actually Atlantis. That there might have been a tectonic plate slip that shifted the continent down south that far. It seems a bit of a far-fetched theory to me but since we are talking about Antarctica ...what is up with that continent?

In 1961 the Antarctic Treaty System was executed, which currently has fifty-four parties. The treaty sets aside Antarctica as a scientific preserve, establishes freedom of scientific investigation, and bans military activity on the continent. Why? What is so special about a frozen continent at the South Pole? Something is amiss with Antarctica. Even Hitler made expeditions to Antarctica, and he was big into the occult. It is thought there is alien technology inside the frozen continent that the military knows about. If you ever look at it on Google Earth, there are oddities.

Back to Atlantis. Some believe it is in the Mediterranean. Some believe it might even be in the Bahamas based on statues and an underground city found. But maybe it was smack in the middle of the Atlantic. How Plato outlined the main city center was extremely detailed. Wherever it was, there are a large number of people who believe it did, in fact, exist.

There are two main viewpoints to Lemuria and Atlantis. One is that Lemuria came first, then that civilization fell, then the Atlantans rose up. This theory supports the Root Races concept by Blavatsky. The second theory is more along the lines of a repeat of Mars and Maldek, where Atlantis was getting power hungry and, in an effort to control Lemuria, blew it up using something like the Hadron Collider and accidentally backfired and caused a catastrophic event at Atlantis. Both continents sunk into the sea. It is said that this ascension is really about the karmic cycle ending between the Lemuria and Atlantan souls lost in that original catastrophe. This topic is a fun one to root around on.

One last Atlantis point. I found it interesting that in the Atlantis tales, scientists and spiritual leaders were at odds. The scientists were doing all sorts of experiments and creating half breeds. Half human, half animal creatures. Then you move forward in time to the Egyptians and all the half-breed creatures shown in their hieroglyphs. I always wondered, where did those come from?

WORKING THROUGH DISCERNMENT

So how do you work through whether something is a trap or if someone involved is legit or not? It is a tricky thing. But there are some hard rules I was able to use as key determinants.

Is the person operating from their ego or their heart?

When dealing with a topic, remove all your preconceived beliefs and look at it from a new perspective and based on what is being presented.

+ What is the viability of it?
+ What seems possible?
+ What seems not possible?
+ What sends up a red flag?
+ What is a new piece of information that is either intriguing or perplexing?
+ Go look up more things based on what your intuition guides you to do.
+ Identify things that are disqualifiers based on other related information you know is solid.
+ Identify what resonates with you.
+ Identify what else this new information connects with.
+ Identify if the conflicts in the information you have are because of your preconceived beliefs or because you just need more information before the scales can tip in one direction.

+ If you have that kind of impasse, then put those two thoughts on a rainy-day shelf in your mind to wait for the day a new piece of information connects to it and how.
+ When dealing with individuals and their motives, it's a fine line between not holding someone to their past, and yet their past is a possible indicator of their present and future behavior.
+ Are there eyebrow-raising comments or actions in their past that are in conflict with words they use?
+ What do their motives appear to be?
+ What do they gain by sharing this information?
+ Is it morally sound?
+ What are the overarching belief systems this person espouses?
+ Are they ruled by their ego or their heart?
+ Do they appear sane?
+ Do they appear logical?
+ Do they appear to have a duty to inform?
+ Can you dispute their viewpoint not defaulting to your social programming mechanisms to do so?
+ Do they display traits of compassion, kindness, and a collective ideology of equality for all?
+ What facts do they have to back up what they say?
+ What is their vibe?
+ What resonates with you and what doesn't, and why?

Be critical. Flush it out. Don't accept anything at face value.

For more info on extraterrestrial stuff, I suggest looking into these: *Unacknowledged, Close Encounters of the Fifth Kind, Cosmic Secret, Above Majestic.*

CHAPTER 18

WHERE DO WE GO
FROM HERE

I know I just dropped a lot of heavy shit on you. I also know what that feels like because it is how I felt discovering it so closely packed in my timeframe. That is why this book is sprinkled with clues. Little Easter eggs of words to help you with key word searches. I struggled trying to sort through this mixed in with the information in the following Healing Chapters. But I found my way through, and I know you can too. Use this as a springboard but remember to always question everything.

At this point, be asking yourself this question. Why does this even really matter? Aren't we circling back to that beginning-of-time question of, what is the meaning of life? Of our lives?

Honestly … yes.

I said in the beginning that the biggest deception about you will be uncovered.

+ By now you have woven through the thread that religion has been used to mentally control the masses from realizing their divine potential as humans.
+ That governments and conquerors have hidden or rewritten history to their liking.
+ That we are effectively in a soul cycle reset tied to the days of Atlantis and Lemuria. Required to do a 26,000 year karmic ascension cycle.
+ That psychic abilities are something all of us have to varying degrees. Utilizing these abilities, such as telepathy, brings us closer to reducing deceit and betrayal. Forcing us to evolve as a physical species as well as at a soul level.
+ That humans are not even close to the top of the proverbial food chain of the most intelligent life forms in existence. Our governments are lying about that.
+ There is some higher control mechanism in place with our planet with various intelligent life forms, but for what purpose is unclear to the masses.
+ In order for our souls to get off this planet, we have to complete the ascension process, or we will have to replay it out again on a different planet once this one is toast. Or you can choose at the time of death not to go to the tunnel.
+ We are more connected at a soul and energetic level than we previously realized.

You might be thinking that's interesting, but why should I care beyond my own current existence? It doesn't seem like I can do much to change anything. True, you don't have to care beyond your existence. You do have that choice. But the root I got to. The real big key in all of this and why it seemed so immensely more important came down to one thing. It's nuclear war. Bioterrorism is close behind that as it simply resets what we have achieved ... again, but nuclear war is the big problem. Aside from the horror of what it does physically to all matter on Earth, it goes deeper.

From the beginning of the book, I told you that everything is energy. Your aura is your own personal toroidal field. That is, in fact, your energetic soul. Then I got you comfortable with the idea that your soul lives on and on and on just having multiple physical human avatars and experiences. However, in the event of a nuclear or atomic explosion that impacts a human being, it takes your light energy body of consciousness and effectively shatters it at the nucleic level.

Imagine there are pieces of your consciousness or soul, drifting into a void, unable to collect each other, find each other, and in a state of conscious pain. Imagine if there are billions of humans with thousands of fractals. If you thought hell was on Earth, you certainly won't want to be part of a nuclear explosion reaction at the soul level.

A nuclear explosion on Earth is also not relegated only to Earth. Because we are all interconnected to a larger group of souls energetically, it's kind of like how *Star Wars* talks about tapping into The Force. Physics illustrates how energy can ripple through space and time. Earth has portals to other worlds and dimensions. Those portals also radiate energy to other parts of our universe and possibly into others. Do we really hate each other so much we want to shatter people's eternal souls?

We have been living for many thousands of years in a patriarchal dominated society. The error of Lemuria was having a lack of masculine energy in their culture and not tapping into and balancing that. Theirs was a society of feelings. The error of Atlantis was not tapping into feminine energy, wanting to utilize different energy methods as long as there were no emotions. It was more calculating and controlling. From hypnosis accounts, Atlantis used some type of underwater sonar device that caused earthquakes in the ocean. From there, massive tsunamis wiped it out, and then the island sank. But that wasn't an atomic explosion. Neither was Atlantis. But the souls made a pact to do better. The time is now to start balancing that masculine energy within all of us with the feminine energy that needs to rise. Dissociate the idea of feminine energy with concept of being feminine. Feminine energy is associated with the creative traits of an individual and their ability to emotionally express themselves and be with the flow of the moment. It is heart centered energy. Being feminine is outwardly displaying yourself in a manner that you believe is in line with how the female gender portrays itself. In achieving that balance, we restore ourselves, as well as positively touching others by our improved existence. When you stand in your authenticity as your version of truth, you own your power. You own your voice.

THE TYRANT AND THE PANDEMIC

I wrote all of the previous chapters and the ones to come a year before the pandemic. But this next part is some retrospective after going through a good portion of the pandemic that I wanted to add it in before publishing.

When I think about that Lemuria/Atlantis tale from the book *A Hypnotist's Journey to Atlantis*, it reminds me that Hiroshima and Nagasaki might have been the replay of Lemuria in a way, only worse. Those were atomic bombs. An influx of Starseeds that heard "The Call" to help prevent another Atlantis. An inference that there was a tyrannical dictator during the time of a virus, a quarantine, and a vaccine during Atlantis. Parallels. Apparently, we are at the end of this karmic cycle. That is why there is this Great Awakening. People remembering things about previous lives are coming through. People are realizing the world isn't how it should be. People realizing why nowhere feels like home. People are realizing through technology what is happening in other parts of the world and are outraged. Realizing the problems we face are really global socio-economic problems our leaders hide behind laws and rules and fancy words as to why they are unable to enact change. There now is a push to break out of the blinders we have been walking around with. Break free from the social programming we received as children rooted in the ideology of ... well, that's what my family has always done or thought, and I never thought to question it.

There was so much emotional and mental horror for a large group of people in 2015. There had been short periods of public outcry. Discontent. But, was that really so different? I don't think so. The energy of the world shifted when #45 took office though, in ways that many people didn't see coming. Some did though. Some were not surprised. When you were in the thick of his reign, it felt awful. Every day was a new day of what the fuck? Constantly questioning your own sanity or thinking you couldn't have heard what you heard. Or shocked that people really took actions that hurt various groups of people. Or that they completely failed to take any action. I remember when he was elected I said to my therapist, maybe this is what needs to happen to really shine a brighter light for people. Sometimes the castle has to crumble to build anew. I did not think it would be a daily shitshow of gaslighting, however.

What happened over the next few years were defining moments for a lot of people. The reigning line had always been "Everyone has their opinion, and we can all get along regardless." I would venture to say that is really a false narrative. Because what we know, is that billions have been silenced or at a minimum, not heard. But a new emerging collective decided to take a stance. We decided that the current issues front and center we were all facing in regards to the financial wealth and employment situations, healthcare, racism, sexism, gender identity were defining lines in the sand in morality. But a morality in which we were rocked when the ego-centric supremist was found within our families and friends. Years of memories and shared experiences no longer mattered. People were just done, and deciding to redefine their tribe of people. I personally think it was a good thing. We saw the ugliest of some of us. We may have known about some. But the depth of it was shocking for a lot of us. I struggled with some people. Distanced myself from some. Others were already aligned, so that was fortunate. There is a way we should all be treated, with compassion and basic respect. It doesn't hurt to be kind, and often it even pays off. We have been pitted against each other for so long we don't know how to come together anymore.

I've had to explain this to my son, not just the situations that were unfolding in the world, but also why. Making sure he understood where both sides were coming from. Even if one of those sides was severely flawed. I know I am not the only parent doing this either. When he came home and told me one of his classmates had a Blue Lives Matter sticker on their computer, we had a talk about it. We had a talk about Black Lives Matter and what each of these things stood for. I also explained certain underpinning events that were occurring to make things look a certain way when actually there were other things in play. Things not easily noticed, like why were the cops caught on camera standing around a pallet of bricks that was on the route of the protest staged later? Seems suspect, right? I explained that his classmate most likely had an immediate family member who was a police officer. So for them, it was personal. That was the kind of life they were being raised in. So their perspective had a different view and one rooted in people they loved and cared for. So be careful judging your classmates at this stage because they really are going with what their parents do or say. Just like he does with me.

I know millions of parents out there have been having these talks with their children. This means the future generations are going to push us in the right direction even further and hopefully tip the balance into a more centered lifestyle. These old white men need to step aside. It's time for a society that honors, respects, and reflects the beautiful cross-cultural identities of our planet. We have already played out these different avatars before. That is the irony here. We don't only live one life. And most of us who have been here for a while, have been all the major ethnicities at some point.

When the discussion floated about a country/global lockdown, I didn't think it would happen. Since when do world governments agree on stopping commerce, and since when does the United States stop for anything. We didn't for swine flu, or Ebola. Not for AIDS when it was spreading in the 80s. But then it did, and very quickly. My first thought was, this is really odd. Something feels off. In fact, something will always feel off about this whole pandemic and global lockdown. I have what I believe, and some of that is still fluid. With that said, I also remember laughing in the beginning. Realizing a lot of people were going to be forced to really sit with their thoughts. Confront those shadow sides of themselves. Wrestle with their demons.

I think sometimes we have so many distractions these days. We forget that we should be able to be comfortable just sitting alone with our thoughts. No matter what those thoughts are. That actively processing the thoughts we invoke does inherently more for growth than reacting to the current mental stimuli in front of you that doesn't require much thought process.

I think we forget that only a hundred years ago, we all did a whole lot of nothing but sitting with our thoughts, whether in the jobs we did back then or when the sun went down. I knew the people who actively meditate were going to be fine. In fact, they were going to be the ones to help anchor the collective scattered energy. The energy, in the beginning, was so heavy too. I felt like I had a rock on my chest for a few weeks straight. I was vibrating and feeling nauseous at points. The empath in me was not doing well, trying to hold my energy the best I could even inside my house.

The pandemic forced us to be in a time out and had to sit in a head-space evaluating our lives again and realizing there is a large group of people who do not have empathy and compassion for others. Did media and social media play a role here? Of course it did. I think we all started out watching Tiger King and the George Floyd Jr. murder by the police. My horror and surprise has simply turned to sadness for many of these people—definitely the few in my sphere. Basically, there are some people that are just never going to get it. It's like watching a broken loop, and it is just sad it is broken and you can't fix it. Is it the mind that is broken or their soul? Who knows. It doesn't really even matter. They are broken, and you just can't fix them. Walk away.

Twenty-first century Americans are no longer the generation of humans willing to sacrifice personal freedoms for the common good. But it does beg the question, what is the line on what to and not to sacrifice of your personal freedoms for the greater good? I'm not sure I've figured out what my stance is on that exactly. It is a tricky line to walk. My hope is that more people will have a turning point moment. Maybe this book is that moment for them. I hope it is because I want everyone to reclaim their soul and create inner peace.

I do know it is going to take a majority of us to transform the hate in the world. To help people let go of their anger. To drop their prejudices. To stop seeing people as immigrants or refugees or deciding who belongs where because some men drew some lines on a map. That we are all humans. All trying to navigate this complicated life the best way we can with the straws we have drawn. We need to support each other. Uplift each other. Let go of the pain. Break free from the restrictive social program-ming structures we were raised with. And see the people in it not as stepping-stones to your personal achievements but instead, a community where we all work together to sustain ourselves and future generations. It's time to let go of the pain in our past. It's time to heal and evolve.

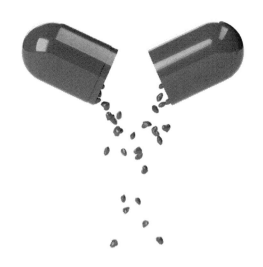

HEALING
CHAPTERS

CHAPTER 19

HEALING YOURSELF OVERVIEW – BODY, MIND, AND SPIRIT

The world we have created is a product of our thinking; it can't be changed without changing our thinking. — Albert Einstein

This section covers processes and understanding for how to heal your mind, body, and spirit in a natural way from trauma. Using ancient knowledge of energy and consciousness healing along with elements from the Earth, you can start the process of healing yourself. This is based on my own experience.

I realized healing was an integral part of the process one must undertake in a soul evolution. I intentionally chose to feel everything physically as I went off my medication so I could experience firsthand what it felt like during every step of the process. Would it work? Would it backfire? I was going to find out. I knew I would have a couple of setbacks which meant increased pain and inflammation. I knew I would have moments I felt like I was plateauing. And in between, then the shifts upward into feeling better.

I knew the healing was not going to be quick—even if I was able to get through the energy and emotional healing relatively quickly, like six months. I knew the physical healing was going to take a couple of years. Maybe longer. So I set my sights on a marathon healing process. I will detail out various things in the coming chapters, but I want to give you an idea of how hard it was for the physical healing. Because it was fucking hard. I also chose to take the hardest of the healing path. So I could write about it, and so I could really pay attention to every nuance in my body. Mentally tracking how I felt and where in my body I felt it, every day all in my head. After I did my energy clearing and amends and all that, I went off all my pain medication. Cold Turkey. I had the sweats, the insomnia, but they only lasted a few days. I started making and drinking daily auto-immune juice. I felt better. Like so much so that two months later I kind of felt like Wonder Woman. I felt like I was back in my twenties.

But then I thought to myself, "I don't know if I am supposed to feel like Wonder Woman in my early forties after being an athlete for so many years." I realized I was ready to wean off my biologic shot. I wanted to see if I could. How bad would it get? I knew it would take some time for the medicine to fully run its course out of me. But hey, I was going to try it. The first two months I was fine with the exception of my kidneys being severely irritated about three weeks later. Terrible pain but didn't feel like kidney stones. Wasn't that bad. It was troubling but, not nowhere near, go to a hospital kind of bad. That pain lasted for months. Then a pain in my mid to upper back formed. I don't even remember the day. If it was more sudden or more gradual. I just remember being in some of the worst pain in my life (not counting my pregnancy experience).

If I was lying in bed, it took everything I had to just go from back to my side or my side to my back. It was this searing pain that felt like someone had speared me, and the pain just … never … stopped. I couldn't sleep more than an hour at a time. I was struggling to do basic household work. Even trying to turn to look over my shoulder while driving the car was sometimes a problem. It was like a muscle spasm that never stops. After about a month of this, I started going to a chiropractor. Then I found a holistic healer. The chiropractic work helped. It was almost like the bones in my spine had collapsed a bit. Pinching nerves, compressing discs. But that shouldn't happen on the medicine, I kept telling myself. In fact, I had never had this horrific pain before. What was this? Going off the medication felt worse than I had been before I went on it a decade prior. Apparently this is the main pain that forms when one has an Ankylosing Spondylitis flare-up. That is what I found out talking with a friend recently diagnosed. I had never had this pain in my life before though. How could this be?

As I started the Rife machine sessions and ionic foot baths, my eyes would get a little dry and almost tired. I didn't feel much beyond that for about six weeks. Then I started to notice feeling a little better. We kept going with the treatments, almost weekly. I still had the pain in my back, but it was smaller. I had a little more movement and was at least somewhat functional. I also was getting massages. After about six months, we introduced using a laser for red light therapy on my spine and SI joints. I noticed an improvement within three days. Still the pain is there, and a feeling like a few of my bones might be fused. I just want my back to crack so bad. When we introduced the laser, we also did some energy work, along with castor oil and heat packs. I did this for a year and a half.

Then the universe rolled some people out and rolled some new ones in. I continued chiropractic and massage along with some energy work.

But I switched to physical therapy. I felt like I just had 20% of the way to go. We did various exercises of mobility to get my back moving. We did core strengthening to get my abs to engage and support my back better. Physical therapy sucks. But it works. The whole time, the knot in my back is still there, just growing smaller and smaller. Changing what the pain feels like. Then one day, we did dry needling and used a tens unit. I was excited. The next day, it felt like we had sprung the trap. The pain in the spot that wouldn't move for two years had moved. Which was good. Except, it didn't go away. It shot higher into my spine and shoulders and gave me sensations I hadn't experienced before. My muscles felt weak holding my head at angles. Felt inflexible, tight, and stuff. But the bad spot was no longer. Over the days to come, it got better. This has taken me over two years to heal. So far, it is worth it.

There are many others that have come before you and done this. You can too. I have faith, anyone can heal who truly wants to. Don't believe me? I got off all my pain medication and my biologic shot I had been taking for a decade for my autoimmune disease. A shot I was otherwise going to be on for the rest of my life. I created energy balls, removed toxic energy, healed generational trauma, rewired the neural pathways in my mind, and DNA got rid of mental shadow images. Changed my diet and worked on having patience in the process of reversing the damage. Because it is a process, and it does effectively feel like your body is going in reverse. So finish this journey with me, and see why they don't want you to know that you can heal yourself. You were never meant to be a crumbling mass of cells. You were meant to be a beautiful ray of sunshine.

When I went off my medication, I was fine for about two months, then I had crippling pain in my mid back so bad I was barely able to sleep or even roll over in bed and sometimes struggled to walk. While writing this book, I was reversing my dis-ease into remission and healed most of the physical damage the dis-ease had caused in my body. I wasn't on medication any longer. Not even ibuprofen. But I got my life back. I did it by focusing on healing myself not just in one area, but in mind, body, soul, and energetically. It wasn't easy to heal emotionally either, as I had a lot of trapped negative emotions. The rest of the chapters walk you through the things I learned and did. Use what I found to heal yourself.

In my past lives, I found out that I was an energy healer, a witch, priestess, a slave, many times over. Not to mention being consistently poor and living in difficult life experiences. It was an interesting revelation that I had not taken that path at all this go-round at life. I had grown up in a medical family and spent thousands of hours in a medical office, but had not chosen a healing path. Even more frustrating was to realize I had so much knowledge in my consciousness on this topic, and yet I couldn't remember it. In fact, I had to relearn what I already knew. Stumbling in the process. Making some mistakes in the process. Frustrated knowing I have a PhD in energy healing, and yet feeling like I woke up in kindergarten and have to relearn it.

I was guided on a specific path in this Awakening. A path that was clear I had to write this book, and I had to make sure it included ways anyone can start healing themself. This is part of my service to others. Steps to take in the process, understanding how all the healing components I found work in conjunction with uncovering everything in the first section simultaneously. You can get your life back no matter the problems.

THE CURRENT HEALTH CARE SYSTEM

I find it interesting that for all the technological capabilities and advancements in science, we have focused on trying to improve longevity for the outside of the body, but not inside. Another example of science focusing on what makes money versus what makes us live longer in a healthier state. The current health care system does not work; between the costs of education for anyone attaining medical training, the lopsided pay system with healthcare workers, coupled with the exorbitant costs to a patient, and the US being the only country in the world where you can go bankrupt over healthcare costs. The pharmaceutical companies and how they push their products down to consumers via advertisements and doctor prescriptions. For-profit healthcare is everything that is wrong with healthcare.

Let me make my view clear, health care is a species issue. It isn't a political party issue although it is associated with such, it isn't a country issue, or a continent issue, it is species issue. Problems in scientific research all center around advancements that make money, not in producing cures or cost affordable treatments that would benefit millions if not billions of people.

The cure to cancer, for example, is not chemotherapy and radiation. How is it that we have millions of extremely intelligent scientists—scientists that have put a man on the moon, created nuclear technology, can clone animals, can map the human genome, but they can't figure out the cure to the most damaging cancers? They can use stem cells to grow things and regenerate. They know what happens with the cells of cancer even to cause the chain reaction of the spread of disease. There are billions of dollars pumped annually into scientific research for this across the globe, and yet, the intelligent scientists and doctors can't seem to figure it out. That holds no logic. The only alternative is that we have unintelligent scientists tackling the cancer problem. That is just not something I can get behind. I can get behind the fact that healthcare is a for-profit system and as a result, anything that does not fall in line with that is not a viable option for research and development. Research is skewed to money projects only.

Several years ago, I went to my doctor and had a test done, and the lab results came back as positive for pre-cancerous cells. I had known this was a possibility at some point, so we had simply been monitoring it year to year. Insurance came back and denied any coverage for the in-office procedure that would get rid of it for good and instead informed me I would have to pay for the procedure costing $750 out of pocket. At the time, I did not have $750 laying around and was literally sitting in that moment thinking, "So, the insurance company would rather I get cancer first, then they will cover for horrific cancer treatment procedures, but an easy procedure that would prevent me from ever getting there and prevent many thousands of dollars being incurred by multiple parties, not interested. That's ridiculous. They want you to be sick because they profit from you being sick. If people are healthy, then they go out of business."

Pharmaceutical sales reps have always made a lot of money by pushing on to doctors the medicine they are selling and giving them samples and perks. Right after I had reconstructive ACL surgery I had a follow up with my doctor for my other knee, which was having problems. Turned out to be overuse of the right knee ligaments due to the physical therapy. He prescribed a topical ointment for the inflammation and told me he had just got back from spending a few years in Germany practicing medicine, and in Europe, they are trying to go to more topical pain medications rather than oral pain medications. When I asked my rheumatologist why she had never mentioned it, she said it was because the insurance companies hadn't covered it previously, so it was expensive.

In case you aren't clear on how new medicines work, let me explain. When a pharmaceutical company comes out with a new drug, it goes under patent. They are able to hold that patent for twenty years ,which means there will be no "generic" option until the twenty years lapses. That means the pharmaceutical company can charge whatever price they want. They justify this by saying they have to recoup the costs of research and development and marketing. So the goal is to try and make as much money as they possibly can before the twenty years is up, which means a price gouge to the patient.

Independent insurance plans won't cover prescription medications that aren't generic or cheap and instead will tell you that your plan simply doesn't cover that, and if they do have a plan that will cover it, the price of your monthly insurance premium is pretty much like having to pay for COBRA coverage when you lose your job. In case you aren't aware, COBRA is an extension of your health insurance when you lose your job. The catch is, you can opt for it, but it will cost you three times the monthly amount you were paying when employed because you are paying the full premium. So you lose your job, have to keep insurance coverage, so you don't get stuck in the pre-existing condition clause when you do land a new job and have new insurance. But you can't afford to pay three times the amount you were paying because you have no job. It is a total circular trap. The only option is to pick up independent coverage for cheap until you get a new job to make sure you cover the gap in insurance. But that insurance doesn't cover much.

There are also some types of doctors that you cannot just make an appointment to go see one. You have to have a referral from another doctor first. Rheumatologists are like that, you can't just call up and schedule an appointment and say you want to run some tests to see if you have arthritis or some other ailment. You have to be referred to a rheumatologist first. As a result, you get dinged with two copays; one for the first doctor and one for the second, usually in the form of a specialty copay. Dental work is the same way. You have to be referred from your dentist to a doctor specializing in oral care for root canals, dental implants, repair work, etc.

Bloomberg does an annual study ranking healthcare systems efficiency across the world using no less than fifty-six countries and seventy-two data points to review. The US has the second-highest per capita spending on health care at $9,536 annually per person. The US ranked fifty-four out of fifty-six nations that met the criteria for the study. The system is so bad that you can be someone who has financially done all the right things. You have built up savings, paid your bills and taxes, and saved for retirement. But the second you get into a catastrophic situation of any kind and insurance either won't cover or will partially cover the expenses, which presents a problem.

You have to drain your finances to pay the bills. You can't claim bankruptcy against those bills until you drain all the financial assets you have. This causes stress and fear. Not just in solving the current predicament, but also because you spent thirty years doing all the right things to have something unexpected happen, and now you are in financial despair you won't ever be able to recover from. Does this seem right to you? Europe and Asia lead the world in healthcare because their approach understands that healthcare is a human problem and it is a larger responsibility to care for the citizens in that country. It really is very simple, except that everyone who stands to profit heavily in healthcare won't be able to make as much money in a subsidized system.

MY HEALTH CARE DISCOVERY

Right after the discovery of my childhood trauma, I also learned that my hot hands were an indication that I had previously been a healer in a former life. The basic premise is that if you were something in a former life, then the DNA encoding of those memories still reside within your energetic aura which means you can access them via your consciousness. You just have to turn within yourself to retrieve it. Aha! Something else about me I had been confused about now having clarity. My awful, sweaty palms I have always had. I just figured it was a hormonal imbalance or something.

I had a realization that fortunately had me turn very quickly in my mindset. The devil may have tried to crush me, but I could undo this damage. I could heal myself. And in healing myself, I could help others figure out how to heal regardless of their energetic psychic abilities. But you have to put in the work. If you want the easy path, then this is definitely not it. It isn't just about healing your body. You have to heal your mind and your spirit. It's a three-part process that all works together, and it takes time.

The lightning bulb moment for me on this goes back to the book *The Emotion Code* by Bradley Nelson—the same book one of the psychics told me to read. I had picked it up and started reading it but only got about a third of the way through. A little frustrated, it seemed he had a million ways to say the same thing. While I understood what he was saying, I still felt like I wasn't quite "getting it." So I put the book down and decided I would pick it up at a later time. About two weeks after the trauma discovery, I had a moment where I was looking at the book and decided to pick it up again. I opened the book at the point I had stopped, read one page, screamed, and threw the book down.

I had been learning about Qigong energy and the chakras. The *Emotion Code Book*, all of a sudden, connected those energy principles and how trauma causes it. The chakras cycle it through, then we don't ground properly, so the toxicity cycles back up the body over and over. The brain sends the body signals to the chakras on the emotional pain in your consciousness and mind and tweak tweak tweak. Dis-ease appears. My abuser hijacked my Root (trust) and (Power) and Sacral (sexual), and Throat (communication) chakras. I was more horrified than ever.

When I read up on that, I realized this is why I have my dis-ease. My dis-ease is an autoimmune issue that is centered in my low back. The cartilage in my sacroiliac joints had eroded out substantially by the time we identified the dis-ease. Like jaws took a chomp out of what should be a smooth arc of cartilage. It also causes severe inflammation. The medicine I (was) on is super expensive, which meant I was always going to be dependent on it, and why I never thought I could be an entrepreneur. I couldn't afford to not have corporate level health insurance because the cost of four shots is about $6,000 a month out of pocket.

At the time of this discovery, I had just landed on the reincarnation topic and discovered I had been a powerful healer in the past. That made me excited. I felt like I had just come out of a swamp, really dirty, and just decided he wasn't going to have power over me anymore, and I was getting rid of this garbage. It no longer suited my purpose and I have the ability to heal myself. If I healed before, I could heal again. I just have to remember how.

I want to be clear, the only person that can heal your mind and spirit … is you. They can heal your body, but not your mind or your spirit. To heal your body to be in unity with the healed spirit, you either need to have previously been a healer, or you need to learn how to in this lifetime, or you need a professional healer to engage. Some people say, all you need is you. But I don't agree with that. If someone parked a shiny new car in front of you and said, "Here you go." If you have never driven before, how do you know how to drive? The tools at your disposal and when to use them, what the rules are for operating the roads, so you are following them? You may have seen other cars on the road and others driving the car you are in, but if you haven't done the research, the practicing, then you don't know what you are doing, and you will make unnecessary mistakes. Mistakes that can hurt you or the person you are trying to help. Healing is no exception to the Principle of Best Intentions and the Rule of Unintended Consequences.

CHAPTER 20

THE DARK NIGHT OF THE SOUL—SHADOW WORK

While you don't need to be triggered into going through the Dark Night of the Soul in order to start physically healing yourself, the truth is if you don't fix the root problems emotionally, then the problem will come back. In one's path of Awakening, you go through what is called the Dark Night of the Soul. In order to come through this on the other side is the healing component of this process in your transformation. So what is the DNOTS?

It is when you bump up against a core belief system you have held and realize it is falling apart. And in that falling apart, it has tangles that stretch and reach to other areas of your life and other people involved in them. It is a type of dying off of your old self and a new self being installed. It is an emotional ride into the recesses of your inner self. You often feel depressed, confused along with a lot of other low vibrational emotions. Your thinking process changes on some core idea. This process of evolvement is called Shadow Work. Shadow Work is simply, working through your own demons and working through your own conflictions to get to clarity.

This transformative process led me to the understanding that evil is a religious concept, not a scientific one. Whatever it is that has led you to this point. It was for a reason.

I was not expecting to tumble onto the path of a spiritual Awakening. At each step of this process, it felt overwhelming. The layers upon layers that kept adding to it. The horror of information that connected to each other that I wanted to deny every time I tried to find an endpoint to my question, but why? Never feeling like I was finding one and everything being connected like I stepped out of a high-rise building for the first time and looked up, never realizing until that moment there had been a multitude of floors above me. It is a lot to process and sit in. You constantly fight against the dichotomy of your mind. How it has formed its information since existence by the programming of everyone around you and in control of the things you need. Yet, the reality of new information intertwining has you looking at things from a perspective you never imagined previously. This is where you have what is called cognitive dissonance. Cognitive dissonance is when your mind is holding two opposing points of view simultaneously.

As your old way of thinking starts to mentally tear apart and a new way of thinking is formed. There will be times it feels hopeless, pointless, fruitless, fearful, horrific, and overwhelming. But in between those moments, you will have a few things that make you smile and help you come out on the other side and into the light.

You deal with the deepest part of the shadows in your life. Have an unnatural fear of something? That's an issue to look into further. If nothing in this lifetime, then it is tied to something in a previous one. Your life going to shit? The universe is trying to show you that you are on the wrong path, and you need to make different choices or view things differently. The more you fight it, the worse it will get. That means you have to make changes, and if you don't make those hard changes, you will stay in the swamp you have been operating in for the rest of your life. That may mean you have to cut off family, friends or end a relationship.

You drop your preconceived views on religion, politics, the world, and even your role in it. There is a difference between what your heart feels and what your soul tells you. When those two things are in conflict with each other, it hurts even more. That is what the DNOTS is about. A splitting of what you believed in that mentally fractures your psyche, creating neurons to fire differently, which then process situations differently than before.

While an awakening has loads of shadow work (DNOTS), at some point, the general awakening ends. The shadow work, however, might be a lifetime pursuit. Awakening is about learning the truth of all this. Shadow work is the work you have to do on your inner self to heal, resolve and come to terms with. Even if you think you don't have any work to do, you have work to do. Just because you have been to a therapist for years working on yourself, if you didn't realize all this other stuff, you would be right. But this opens up a whole new layer of understanding.

The famous psychiatrist Carl Jung coined the term Shadow Work as the dark side of our personality that we can't see in ourselves. Or maybe choose not to see. They are the unexamined or disowned parts of ourselves that don't have anywhere to go even though we try to cast them out or aside or repress them. A lot of this is wrapped up in our unconscious mind, which can often be in the driver seat without us consciously aware of that. I highly suggest looking into Jung's research on shadow work or any other writers that might have interpreted it into a working format for you to understand.

There are different areas of shadow work to tackle. The overarching idea is that anything that you feel: shame, guilt, apathy, grief, fear, or anger, needs to be explored. This is where doing timeline reviews is important.

Dealing with one's emotional and mental well-being is a relatively new change in society's ideology. I remember asking my parents to send me to a psychologist when I was seventeen years old because, clearly, something was wrong with me after two suicide attempts. They said no. After much arguing, they eventually came to the idea that I could talk to our priest, and if he felt I should see someone, then they would consider it. No. I didn't need to talk to a priest to know I needed to talk to a professional mental health counselor. Their argument was that everyone in town would know, and then I (they) would be viewed with this stigma. My argument was that a psychologist had to adhere to the same privacy and confidentiality oaths as did my stepfather for his work. And if none of us in that room said anything to anyone, then who would even find out? I've seen two different therapists in my life. Both were my choice and both for different reasons at that point in time. Majorly helpful to me in my journey.

EMOTIONAL TRIGGERS

Emotional triggers are one way to identify some of those, and I covered that in the Managing Being an Empath and Intuitive Chapter. Guilt and shame are situations you have endured. Maybe you were homeless or made it big only to lose it all. The situations are plentiful. What do you have that you feel shame and guilt about? Whatever that is, it needs to be addressed. Shame relates to yourself, whereas guilt revolves involves awareness that our actions have hurt someone else. Depending on your situation, there are different ways of dealing with it. You could sit in the knowledge of the big picture and understanding that these are just experiences, and you agreed to be on this planet. So the only person you can truly hold accountable is yourself. But if you don't work through these and own your role in them, then you are doing what is called "spiritual bypassing".

SPIRITUAL BYPASSING

Spiritual bypassing is where you use spiritual ideas and practices to avoid facing your unresolved emotional and psychological wounds. It's basically like in *The Lego Movie* when they are singing "Everything Is Awesome," but everything wasn't really awesome. There will be times that you face loss, you will grieve, feel anger, witness injustice, see things that need changing and recognize that the world around us is not "Good Vibes Only." That by not acknowledging the shadow side and only sitting in a "Love and Light" state, that we aren't learning how to balance ourselves properly and work through those emotional experiences. Humans are meant to feel. They are meant to have emotional experiences that test and challenge us. If every human being throughout time used the spiritual bypassing mechanism, there would be no improvements in human rights, or equality, or even technological advances. If we all sat back and decided that everyone's life is spouting rainbows, we would lose our ability to improve and to help one another and ourselves.

FEARS

Fears are interesting because there are fears due to events in this lifetime, and then there are fears that are tied to a previous lifetime that you need to clear in this one. On the path to healing and feeling a lighter way of being by vibrating at a higher frequency, you have to face your fears.

Fears in this lifetime would be:

+ Death
+ Surviving a horrific accident but being afraid to get in a car/plane/ boat again
+ Being in a natural disaster and afraid of another one
+ Situations that occurred in this lifetime, repeating themselves in another experience
+ Basic survival and ability to provide for yourself and possibly your family
+ Major life changes

What are your fears, and what are they rooted in? Where did they come from?

When I dropped all ties to any religion and leaned into our divine spirituality and direct connection with Source, I lifted the restrictive programming meant to keep me enslaved to the idea I was born a sinner and thus a piece of shit. I was no longer bound by man's rules on what constituted right and wrong. I actually felt energetically lighter after doing so. When I leaned into reincarnation, then I immediately dropped any fear of death. I dropped fear of the afterlife, dropped fear of loved ones dying and never seeing them again. Any fear of death and its tentacles that I had been holding on to for as long as I can remember just went poof. Like magic.

An unnatural fear of something is when you don't know where it came from or why you have it.

Examples of unnatural fears from previous lifetimes would be:

✦ Are you someone who is deathly afraid of swimming in pools or ponds or lakes or the ocean? If yes, then you probably drowned in a past life. This is an easy one. Start taking swimming lessons to safely bridge that gap in your fear.

✦ Overeating could be a carryover from a previous lifetime where you starved to death. Although it usually has new manifestations in your current lifetime that add to it.

✦ Afraid of needles and getting your blood drawn? Probably lived during a time when there were diseases, and they thought blood-letting would cure them. Brutal methods on blood withdrawal several hundreds of years ago.

✦ Fears of heights, you probably died in a fall or plane

✦ Fear of dogs, you probably were attacked in a previous life.

What are the unnatural fears you have? These are past live indicators, and the only way to clear them is to find out where they stem from. To do so, you need to go into Akashic Records to identify it or go do a past life regression session with a certified hypnotherapist to retrieve them.

When dealing with grief, it is because you lost something or someone you loved. You lost something you didn't want to lose, something you know you won't be able to continue having experiences and memories with. So it is a grieving of the present moment, past experiences, and abrupt end to future possibilities. If it is a person, then lean back into reincarnation. Your grief lessons when you realize they aren't really gone, and there is a good chance you will have another lifetime of experiences with them. You have had many more connections like this with many souls in other lifetimes.

For anger, this is one that probably has a lot of shadow work. What are all the things that make you angry? Why do they make you angry? In this process, what you realize is that these triggers that make you angry are really just mirrors to show you something that needs to be healed. With anger, what you get to is you are angry about something someone else has done, to which you are not able to control the situation or outcome. I highly recommend the work of Abraham (Esther) Hicks or Eckhart Tolle in this area to help you work through your anger issues.

When my Ascension symptoms first started triggering, one of the things that happened was I had a ring on my forehead. It would rise up and feel like it was pulling my skin up. I was reading a lot of stuff on the pineal gland, but nothing was coming up about it being a ring or feeling like a ring on your forehead. But this ring was about two inches in diameter on my forehead. I did come across, however, information on binding rings. What I got to was, someone had placed a binding ring on me, as if a type of curse. I went about two months being angry at this mystery evil consciousness. Only to one day find out, no one else did this to me. I did this to myself. The confusion and horror at that thought. I did it … to myself. It is a humbling moment when again, you have no one else to blame but yourself and the actions you took. The next obvious question was, why would I do that?

Apparently, I married into black magic at one point in a previous life. This fit. I have always identified with witches of the dark ages even before my Awakening. If I put a binding ring on my third eye intentionally, that meant I was in a really bad situation that I saw no way out of. I saw the visions come forth. It made sense. I had no one else to be angry at. I only had myself to reconcile this with. I also had to figure out how to undo the ring. I had to have compassion for that other life. The experiences that I went through in it. The emotional and mental pain I endured led me to such desperation. What I may or may not have known at the time was that I didn't just bind myself in that lifetime. I effectively bound myself energetically from that point forward. It took me about six months of work to clear that ring up.

You will identify the generational curses in your family that you were subjected to. You most likely will realize in looking back that you already cleared some of your negative karma or family generational trauma by not repeating the cycle. That was one of the reliefs I felt, looking back and realizing how I had done that naturally in several situations throughout my life. If you were abused, for example, but as you grew, you did not become an abuser, that is an example of breaking a generational curse or a generational cycle within a family. So if that is you, you can look back with relief, knowing you did not continue to perpetuate the cycle. The buck stopped with you.

Your shadow work with others means you have to step back and analyze the intended person. Is this someone you care deeply about? Is this someone that feels the same way toward you? If not, then there is an imbalance. Depending on who it is, you have to decide how you are going to hold that space with them. Some people are toxic, and you simply need to walk away from them. Some people are simply misguided and stubborn. Is it worth it for you to feel right and justified with that person or to simply sit in your reality of truth?

There are people you walk away from, people you resolve issues with, and people you simply decide you are going to view the world differently and instead work on how you emotionally deal with them if they invoke a triggering situation. Some people you may simply need to set boundaries with. Even if you have never set boundaries with them before, now you do. That might be very hard if you are an adult child that needs to set boundaries with their parents or even an older sibling.

Setting boundaries, taking time for yourself, owning your role in the situations, and how you can improve them moving forward are all ways of respecting yourself and working on self-love. You will often be surprised that after resolving something, you will have a situation that comes around that says, but are you sure? Don't doubt yourself now! If you find yourself in a despairing situation, focus on the motivational spiritual and energy healing quotes, as you will find solace in those during dark times. Once you start clearing all of this, your body starts to alter itself mind, body, and spirit.

HEALING FOR THE VICTIM

TRAUMA

The first step in the healing process for a victim is to identify the trauma and the person who inflicted the trauma. If you know who that is, good. If you don't, you just know something is off or feels wrong, or believe you have a repressed memory, then you need to do an Akashic Reading or a hypnotherapy regression with someone who can help you locate the trauma. Once the trauma is identified, cry it out. Let yourself feel what you need to feel. Don't hold it in to "hold it together," all you are doing is pissing off your body. When you have hit your bottom and are ready to pull yourself back up (it might be a week, a month, or a year even, but I hope not), you are ready to no longer be a victim. This is when you convert from being a victim to being a survivor.

Your next step is to write a letter. There is a ritual in undoing something that was done. You can make that letter whatever you want it to be. It can be your anger and rage pouring out. It can be you expelling the hurt and shame you have felt, whatever you need to purge out this whole experience in order to TAKE YOUR POWER back. This is about taking back your energy and your power and control of your spirit, body, and mind.

Next, you need to think about why you are done with this. Why are you choosing to release the hurt and pain and anger and shame? When it comes up again in an image or a related conversation, what is the reason you will give yourself and be able to repeat, "No, I am done with that. It doesn't serve my best interests." It has to be firm enough that when it happens, you recognize, "This is a shit sandwich, and I don't want to eat it. I don't even want to touch it to throw it away. Someone is in my house, and I want them to leave now."

Find a private space, whatever room makes you most at ease. I think crystals are great for this process, but if you don't have them, again, it is energy and intentions. I highly advise you to pick up some healing candles at least. Read your letter out loud. Cry it out, yell, whatever you need to do to expel what you feel. Release the energy you have been holding inside you. When you are done, burn the letter and clear your energy like I mentioned how to do earlier.

For any kind of trauma, you have to be mentally ready to work through it. Even in doing so, I highly suggest a professional health therapist to help you through the healing process.

SEXUAL ABUSE

On this topic, there are three audiences.

1. The ones actually abused.(Victim/Survivor)
2. The ones who did the abusing. (Perpetrator)
3. The ones impacted secondarily by the abuse and the role they played in it. (Accomplice/Complicit)

To heal from sexual abuse is a hard process that impacts body, mind, and spirit. The order in which you tackle this has to be spirit first, then mind, then body. You can work on all three at once, but proper work leading into it must be done on the emotional side, or else, it simply won't work. Afterwards, a reprogramming by your mind will need to occur over the coming weeks and months.

Sexual abuse is a violation of the mind/body/spirit. Murder is also a violation of the three, but the difference there is, the victim dies and transitions on to reincarnate again. With sexual abuse, the victim now has to live their life still.

If someone has been abused as a child, it is more likely that they will suffer abuse again. This is known as revictimization.

Long-term effects of abuse and neglect include:

+ Emotional difficulties such as anger, anxiety, sadness, or low self-esteem
+ Mental health problems such as depression, eating disorders, post-traumatic stress disorder (PTSD), self-harm, suicidal thoughts
+ Problems with drugs or alcohol
+ Disturbing thoughts, emotions, and memories that cause distress or confusion
+ Poor physical health such as obesity, aches, and pains
+ Struggling with parenting or relationships
+ Worrying that their abuser is still a threat to themselves or others
+ Learning difficulties, lower educational attainment, difficulties in communicating
+ Behavioral problems including anti-social behavior, criminal behavior

Because I believed in the Starseeds theory, I rooted my acceptance of my role in this by understanding I signed up for this shitshow. I only have myself to blame for these experiences. I mean, I'm not saying I opened my heart to my abuser with peace, love, and light because there are negative entities at play here that we are battling. Not my style. I'm a justice person. There was a point I wanted to make his spirit shake. To tell him I knew what he did to me. Even as simple as that.

However, for my own health and well-being I chose to never go into his physical presence again, nor have any real contact moving forward.

Because that can trigger things to become a new energy connection to that person. In the final days when he was dying, however, I did wish for peace in his soul. Growth and evolution as well. He was in pain, dying from cancer. While I have strong feelings about this man, I don't want anyone to be in pain.

Additionally, just because you have cleaned your energy, don't think it can't be tainted again by a specific person. I highly advise if you are still subjected to situations with someone who is your abuser that you find a way to exit the relationship for your own health and well-being. It may have residual consequences to others, but you have to walk your path, and safety and security is as important as food and water.

To work through your mind, I highly suggest speaking with a professional mental health advisor, as sexual abuse has tentacles that reach into almost every area of your life. Your personality, impacts to relationships, thoughts of self are just a few areas. And it is a very deep process to work through.

CONFRONTING AN ABUSER

This is a delicate thing to do and a very personal decision to make. You have to judge the character of the person in question and the situation. Was it a horrible judgment on their part and normally out of character, or is this just an asshole with no regard for others? For me, I realized I was dealing with a psychopath, and psychopaths do not behave in the manner you expect. They are highly unpredictable and are unrepentant because they refuse to believe they did anything wrong and are willing to lie and believe their own lies even as a result. You have to identify a battle that will not be won and simply walk away from it. I chose to walk away from mine, but that might not be the choice you make. If you do decide to confront your abuse, I highly suggest you look for an individual that specializes in this sort of thing to help you through it and to be a pillar of support for you in this process.

Once you have worked through the mental issues associated with the trauma and clearing your energy of it, the next is to work on healing your body. Work through what you need to do to align your chakras and change the cellular structure your body has been operating from with diet, meditation, and all the rest.

CANCER/AUTOIMMUNE DISEASES

I have an extreme view on cancer and the healthcare industry but auto-immune is in my alley. The root of all disease is the inflammation of a damaged cell. Scientists know this. They have been fighting cancer for at least the last seventy years. So in the last seventy years, with millions of brilliant scientists and billions of dollars in research, you want me to believe they are just so damn stumped on how to cure cancer that doesn't rely on injecting poison into you? That just doesn't make sense.

Cancer cells fester because of an extreme trauma that has trapped negative emotional energy inside the body. The emotions radiate throughout the chakras, because we don't physically ground anymore. The negative energy then recycles throughout the body, creating a looping cycle that over time just does more and more damage. Additionally, while we skew our energetic currents from not grounding, we also have changed our dietary habits to be more acidic rather than alkaline.

Diseases can't thrive in an alkaline environment. You have to identify your traumas. A trauma can be sexual abuse or assault, violence, emotional or verbal abuse, a car accident, witnessing an act of violation against another human being, near-death experiences that are still traumatizing, etc. Figure out what the trauma is. Following what I told you about releasing negative energy from your energetic aura and body. From there, the mind will start to heal the body.

DOMESTIC VIOLENCE

Part of childhood trauma could be simply witnessing the trauma of another person. If you were a child that witnessed a parent or sibling be abused, then you may have feelings of fear, anger, and guilt associated with it. Maybe you believe somehow or some way you could have stopped it, or reported it. Or it could be that you were the victim of abuse. It doesn't even matter if that abuse occurred as an adult. If it did, it still is a violation against your mind, body, and soul and needs to be worked through. Self-esteem and self-confidence issues will most likely be in play here.

I cannot stress the importance of ensuring you manage your health with licensed health care professionals that understand the mechanisms of the mind and what needs to be done in the interest of one's health in overcoming issues rooted in repeated patterns due to psychological trauma.

ADDICTION/EATING DISORDERS

Addiction and eating disorders are psychologically rooted. Feeling you are not good enough or have so much pain that the tradeoff gives you pleasure or satisfaction of sorts. Beholden to a fear of something you hold onto tightly. Addiction is a way to escape from the reality of your life. Eating disorders have self-love at the root of the problem. You lack self-love, and you feel an area of your life is out of control, so as a self-defense mechanism, you create a knee-jerk reaction to the lack of control and an eating disorder is formed and then nurtured. Excessive eating also appears as remnants of past lives where you previously starved. It is the counter experience to starving.

PTSD/ANXIETY/DEPRESSION

PTSD is an energy imbalance due to being in a situation that rocked your consciousness core, and you experienced pure fear or horror. Your heart chakra has been rocked to its core and you are left with a hole you are desperately seeking to fulfill. Depression is rooted in the idea of sadness of something in the past.

Whereas anxiety is rooted in fear of something in the future either happening or not happening based on past experiences. When you have anxiety, you can feel the energetic imbalance inside you. Sometimes it feels like your heart is racing, when in fact, there is no change in the actual rhythm of your heartbeat. This is what you feel when you have a panic attack. Like you are struggling to breathe, and your heart rhythm is heightened. With anxiety, the idea that we don't know what will happen in the future and the past has been hard, which makes it difficult to trust. Trust ourselves really that we can make it through whatever is thrown our way. But you can. I mean, up to this point in your life, you have survived 100% of your worst days.

Whatever the choices or decisions and outcomes that played out. Maybe you had a hand in the decisions, or maybe you didn't. Understand that the experiences you had, no matter how painful, were ones you agree to experience in your blueprint. View them in a light where you find something you can pull as a learning lesson. Then let go of what you are holding on to. Religion taught us that we were born with sin, but really, we aren't born with sin. The human experience is not one that is meant to be an exercise in perfection, even though we are constantly trying to achieve it. We all have challenges we have to overcome. So let go of regret, sadness, frustration, anger, shame, hate.

HEALING FOR THE VICTIMIZER

On the path to karmic clearing, this is key. If you were someone who victimized another person in this lifetime, then the only way to clear this in this lifetime is to essentially atone for it. To that other person. This isn't something that you can go to church, weep to the priest privately, confess my bad God, say five Hail Mary's, and exit stage right to the waiting Ferrari. If you do not atone for your actions to the person whom you violated, then in the next lifetime, you will either be in a situation being abused yourself, or you will have to be a player involved in someone you love's abuse. Is that what you want? There is no further healing that can be done for you if you fail to do this. Even if you decide to skip this step and try to attempt the healing protocols, your spirit knows, your mind knows, and your body is communicated to accordingly. It just won't work. When you die, there is a good chance your spirit has to go through some cleansing as well. A violation against another spirit's free will and choice is the line not to cross. And it's a pretty easy line to follow.

I highly suggest that in your path to resolve your errors, you seek professional mental help.

HEALING FOR RESIDUAL PLAYERS INVOLVED

If you are a secondary party to abuse, or maybe you are a parent who didn't protect your child, or a sibling or friend that refused to believe someone close to you was abused and realize you failed to support someone in their time of need. Just as in the case of an abuser, you have to accept the role you played, seek forgiveness and then see what kind of support you can now provide that person. From there, you have to work through your own shadow and come to an acceptance of your choices. You don't have to love your past decisions. Simply understand where you went wrong and why you made the choices you did and then put them to rest. We are all growing and learning in our lifetimes. This is a growth process you can achieve. If you don't, then you will let shame and grief keep their grip on you.

Guilt. That is the main emotion that weighs down heavily on the brothers, sisters, mothers, fathers, aunts, uncles, friends, or whoever that either were unaware of a situation occurring or may have been aware but refused to acknowledge or investigate or intervene. Guilt is a bag of heavy trash you carry around that serves no purpose other than to weigh you down. Whereas fear can be both a motivator and an inhibitor, pending the situation and the point of view. Guilt centers around a personal failure. A failure to recognize, a failure to believe, a failure to make the best decisions, and the recognition in hindsight, and the complete inability to go back and undo it. Any time one's version of reality is put to the test and then found out to not be the view they believed, it causes a split within oneself. It starts to create repetitive negative loops. The person spirals into how their role led to or allowed a horrific violent act that was a violation of another human's body, mind, and spirit. A human you love. At the root of this is deception. Someone deceived you, and they did it to another human being you care for.

So how do you resolve this and drop the guilt? The healing process here centers around the situation. Remember the discussion about blueprints and the Akashic Records? This is where you have to go. Understand if you are in this situation, it means you were in this type of situation before, in a previous life. You thought being a party to this was bad. Wait until you find out some more bad stuff. Maybe you were the person who was abused in a previous life. Maybe you were the abuser in a previous life, and in this lifetime, you are to be a bystander that has no ability to prevent or resolve the situation but has to understand how horrific it is to learn the other side of the equation as to why this is so horrible. The truth sets you free, even in all its ugliness.

In order to come to terms with this, you realize this is all part of a karmic cycle. Even if the person abused is not able to come to the same point you do, that is not for you to solve for them. Maybe not even in this lifetime. If you have to come to terms with it and get to a place of acceptance that this was a larger part of a plan where this was an experience you agreed to at a high level to endure and grow from. If you don't grow and learn from it in this lifetime, then when you die and come back, guess what? You will have to go through this again, and again, and again until you learn from it. What is the lesson? Well, you have to work through that in your own personal situation, but at a high level, a violation against another person's well-being is not acceptable behavior for a human to exhibit.

There are boundaries that should not be crossed. If one's previous beliefs led them astray, then they need to review their beliefs to identify the contradiction and change them. If their trust in someone led them astray, what was it in developing those bonds of trust that might have been an indicator? If none, then there is nothing there for you to resolve. Sometimes, sexual predators are so sly, that they can convince almost anyone that kind of behavior insinuated at them is simply unbelievable. You were deceived. Sometimes when we are deceived, there just weren't any clear-cut signs to indicate something was amiss. Sometimes it is the situation that we are in that we look back and say, well, could I have changed it?

For example, maybe you were a single parent struggling financially, and daycare had to go in a certain direction. It wasn't your first choice, or maybe you thought it worked out great for you in the moment. When you look back, you may realize, crap, there really just isn't anything I feel I could have done differently at the time to prevent that. Or I looked at all my options and felt this was the best one because of these reasons. That is okay. Again, that is recognition and acceptance that the situation just was what it was meant to be. Even if not ideal. Your life was not meant to be perfect. It was meant to be riddled with experiences. And those experiences are what allow you to grow and expand by the emotions that you go through on your journey based on the corresponding choices you then make as well. That is part of the healing process.

In this process, I suggest you write a few letters—one to the survivor and one to yourself. You write whatever you need to say to the survivor and. At the end, burn the letter while stating that you are releasing the pain of this situation from your energy and mind as it no longer serves a purpose with you. That you are sending healing energy in the form of love to the victim. That you hope they can conquer their demons and you only want the best for them and moving forward, you will be a pillar of strength and positive energy for them to help light the journey for them to heal. When you need to be that pillar of strength for them, you will find the calm from within because it is your role to be a support player.

The second letter is to yourself. This is probably the harder of the two, you have to forgive yourself of ... everything. Simply accept the situation as part of a larger blueprint, one that you infuriatingly cannot remember the whole scope of, but you agreed to the possibility of this. You can write out all your anger, your pain, shame, guilt, anything you need. Don't hold it back. You need to do this in a ritual because that way, it is part of a moment in time that you intentionally stopped and said, "Today I change the timeline. Today I shift away from the destructive patterns that have led to my physical, mental, and spiritual decline. Today I take back my power over myself from this situation as it no longer serves a purpose for me."

The survivor is the one with the most pain, so remember to keep that sensitivity at the forefront while dealing with your own trauma.

SPIRITUAL BLOCKS/ENERGETIC CORDS/MANTRAS
Spiritual blocks are when you have self-doubt, limiting beliefs, don't trust your intuition, and don't feel in alignment with your life in general. Like ... this wasn't the plan. Not even knowing what the plan was, just that this was not it. Work through your emotional triggers to see what your spiritual blocks are.

Energetic cords are connections you have with people you intertwine with. Even acquaintances or people in a store create an energetic residue that intertwines in your aura. Words are thoughts with intentions. Words without intention are meaningless. In essence, your words are spells or vows. That is why it is called "spell-ing." I guess that makes us all witches by definition. When you are ready to release negative or controlling energy, then saying these will help to cut the cords that bind you to other people. There are other revocation mantras you can say, but you need to be careful what the full intent of that means. Any clearing of other systems or programs you revoke, you need to do so for all timelines and dimensions, not just the one you are currently in. Remember, this is a soul type of clearing, not a human body clearing.

I hereby void all contracts that were entered into against my free will. My energy cannot be used to feed negative systems, entities, or consciousness without my consent, and I am revoking any previous consent given.

If I have harmed anyone in any way, either knowingly or unknowingly, through my own confusions, I ask their forgiveness, and I send them healing energy of love to assist them in their path of evolutionary consciousness.

If anyone has harmed me in any way, either knowingly or unknowingly, through their own confusions, I forgive them. And if there is a situation I am not yet ready to forgive, I forgive myself for that and ask for compassion to flow through me so I can get to that place.

For all the ways that I have harmed, negated, doubted, belittled, judged, or been unkind to myself, I forgive myself and have compassion for all that each of my souls and bodies have endured.

I declare that I am more than good enough. I am infinite consciousness. I am a sovereign being in charge of my own free will, and I hereby reclaim my divine power. I declare a new form of spiritual and physical cleanliness starting now.

If you need to energetically sever cords with a specific person, then use the following. I suggest you do this when you do the letter writing and reading and burning exercise discussed previously. Ensure you surround yourself in a bubble of protection first and clear your energy. Envision this cord between you and the other individual. Then cut it with a knife or scissors you visualize.

I hereby cut the energy cord connecting myself to [insert name]. I return all energy of [insert name] currently in my energy field to them. I recall all energy currently intertwined in [insert name]'s energy field and require it is returned to me in a clear state. The experiences we shared are in the past and have no bearing on my future. If this person ever invokes a new energy cord to reconnect to me, my aura will deny entry and connection. I do not give permission for that energy to penetrate my energy field moving forward. If any negative thoughts are sent to me from this person, then that energy will rebound off my aura, and the energy will return to [insert name]. I release, restore and renew my energy field.

It is important to understand that if you have been a victim of abuse of any sort, then the energy cords need to be severed. This will alleviate the telepathic connections between the two of you. Additionally, by using a rebound on your aura and sending it back, you are not invoking a curse upon that person. You are not creating more karma to deal with in the future. You simply are stating what your energetic boundaries are and are redirecting the original energy sent to ensure your health and well-being.

CHAPTER 21

AWAKENING VS ASCENSION SYMPTOMS

While the Dark Night of the Soul is about death, the spiritual Awakening is about rebirth. I will be honest, if I did not go through the physical symptoms of resistance energy purging and then actually having the mental connections I was having that led to physically help me heal; I would have had a hard time understanding someone else describing it to me, and I surely would have raised an eyebrow at the story. But what I found in my journey, is that not only was I not alone in this but there were also thousands if not millions of people that were experiencing the same kind of Awakening like described in this book and at about the same time. Some already had, some had been for years, but every day more and more people were engaging and coming to terms with the same things.

Synchronicity. Activation Codes. Aches and pains in areas that made no sense, intense fatigue at odd times, and more. If it wasn't for this reason and seeing so many with questions, expressing the same feelings and desires, I wouldn't even have written this book. I would have just sat in my little weirdness. But lots of people were also experiencing similar physical/mental/emotional changes too.

Ascension symptoms are the actual physical, energetic changes in your body that force you to release lower vibrational energies to prepare your body to vibrate at a new frequency. There are many physical symptoms of Awakening that one experiences, but not everyone goes through the same symptoms. For example, one of the big ones is ringing or buzzing in the ears. I never had buzzing in the ear other than the pain of the ear implant I discovered that started vibrating when I started waking up.

I noted in the Akashic Records Chapter that my first resistance energy purge started immediately after my energy aligned in the knowledge of my own truth. I went into seven hours of feeling like I got hit with the flu out of nowhere. Immediate headache, vomiting, and sweating but feeling cold. It was a massive amount of resistance energy that I had been holding onto, forcefully releasing itself out of my body once my mind was now in alignment. It was these physical symptoms I experienced that ran the full wheel of emotions over the next several days and cycled them in and out and all around. This led me to no explanation but Ascension Symptoms.

Aside from the emotional aspects, you will deal with in an Awakening of shock, horror, grief, sadness, and others, the physical side is different. Physically you may experience fatigue, achiness, tightness in areas, feeling like one of your chakras is pulsating (when the heart chakra is opening, the center of your chest will pulsate and feel like it might explode), pinprick tingles, fogginess in the head, and a host of other things. Your diet will start to change naturally. Many people either stop eating meat all together or significantly reduce their meat intake as well as processed foods for a more plant-based diet. Another common one is waking up around three a.m., which is when the veil between the humans and the paranormal is the thinnest. That is why it is called the Witching Hour.

One of my oddities was around three p.m. I would hit a wall all of a sudden and needed a nap. My body would just shut down, and I would fall over right there and be forced to take a nap. It wasn't something I could fight or just drink some caffeine and be good. Additionally, I was sweating all the time like I was running a marathon constantly. I sweated so much that I was constantly changing my clothes and bedsheets for two months straight. Water intake is crucial during and after your Awakening as your body is energetically transforming itself to vibrate and resonate at a higher frequency. Physically you will feel like something is seriously wrong with you that you can't explain. Emotionally you will feel like you are having a psychotic break while simultaneously feeling clear and like the same person you were yesterday. It is quite the dichotomy.

Increased sensitivity to the plight of animals (and our plant food source) will often occur and goes hand in hand with the lack of desire to eat animals anymore. It is said that you absorb the energy of what you eat. Plants have been mapped to energetically vibrate at certain frequencies. So plant-based diets will have a healthier energy vibration, whereas animals will bring with it the energy from how it was treated. If it was treated poorly, then the low vibrational trauma energy trapped within the animal will transfer itself to you when you ingest it. As a result, you most likely will see changes in your weight as your diet changes. You might get some form of skin rash or an outbreak of bumps or acne. This is often toxins trying to be released/expelled from your body.

Your senses will also shift. I had picked up an increased sensitivity to sound and light a year or two before my Awakening. Loud or sharp sounds seem amplified and harsher than they used to be. Your head will have different sensations that they haven't really had before and can't explain what they are—tingles in certain places like your forehead or top of the head, for example. Your intuition will increase, and your sixth sense of emotional feeling grows. For some people, they start to see things they didn't see before. Maybe symbols, patterns, or colors in and around things/people or in the sky.

You also may be prone to energy surges where you feel energy coursing through you in a way you hadn't before. For me, I had slightly the reverse because I had always been operating in a high-energy surging state. So the surges that people have noted experiencing in their Awakening, that is what I felt my entire life. So for me, it was about bringing my energy back to a zero-point field of balance. You might also experience electronics malfunctioning oddly or lights flickering due to your own energetic changes. I had electronics dying on me all about the same time.

Many people will experience more vivid dreams or dreams like they have never had before. For me, I haven't dreamed consistently in the last two decades. There are others like me and for the ones that are, ignore the people that tell you that everyone dreams. Your brain might be active, but that doesn't mean you are actually dreaming. You might actually be astral projecting in your sleep, for example.

Like I said, this is not the full list, and not everyone has the same experiences. But whatever you do experience, understand it is part of your personal awakening mechanism and that it is not permanent. Well, some of them are permanent, like the things you see or the dreams, astral projection abilities, energy shifts, but others like sweating—no you won't be sweating forever.

You will change your viewpoint from things being coincidences to things being synchronicities. You will start connecting things in ways you never did before, and you will start viewing situations differently. You will even look back at your life and start seeing synchronicities in areas you had discounted as coincidental.

While my son has not experienced the Ascension Symptoms, he is awake. After two months of being slammed with downloads and energy purges, dealing with emotional and physical changes, I could feel myself coming out of this tunnel. I felt I owed it to my son to have a little talk about what I was going through. I knew he was a little concerned even though I had been telling him I would be okay and that everyone goes through rough patches in life. During one of my energy readings, I had inquired about my son, and I had been told they saw him pushing something down internally. I knew I had to have a talk with him at some point to see what he knew.

I was nervous. I didn't know how it was going to go. I was just going to give him a real lightweight primer. Hopefully, nothing that would really scare him. I already knew something was up with him that he remembered a couple of things from a previous life without realizing it. So hopefully, this wouldn't be too weird. I don't remember exactly how I started it. I only remember the point pretty quickly after where I defaulted to my typical direct self and said, "So you know aliens are real right? And we are the aliens."

He had been standing and suddenly froze in his motion and looked at me. It was a look consisting of two thoughts. First, so YOU know? Second, should I admit this, it feels like a test?

Reincarnation a minute later, he went all in and said he remembers bits of past lives. I mentioned spirit guides, and he tells me his popped out a few years ago just to let him know he was there. I asked how often he had talked to him, he said not too often, only a couple times, shifting his eyes and not looking at me. He had been apparently talking to him a lot more than that after I started asking more questions. He even knew how to close his mind and quiet it to hear.

This whole thing lasted about fifteen minutes, and he was calm the entire time. Like we were simply having a factual conversation, and I was the one who apparently had been in the dark the whole time and he wasn't. I, on the other hand, walked out of the room completely freaked out and having another mind-bender of thoughts. As if this wasn't crazy enough for me, my son was smack in the middle of being awake and trying to close it down. I couldn't let that happen. But I had gotten to him in time. In fact, if you had talked to him for ten minutes about aliens and ten minutes about religion, he would have looked at you quizzically about religion and not the aliens. He has been able to tell me about things he sees or remembers, and it has been pretty cool.

If you have a child, maybe ask them new questions and see what they tell you. You might be surprised by their answers. Encourage them to remember and stay creative. Ensure they know that there are good and bad voices, and to make sure and only allow the good ones nearby and send the bad ones away. If you have grown children, try to think back to when they were under the age of eight and if they told you anything that seemed really odd. Did they have an imaginary friend? Maybe that imaginary friend wasn't so imaginary after all.

CHAPTER 22

MANAGING BEING AN EMPATH AND INTUITIVE— CHANGING YOUR SCRIPTS

Following from the earlier chapters on what an empath is, I would say there are two kinds of empaths and three important steps in your evolution as an empath.

The two types of empaths are structured and unstructured. An unstructured empath is an empath who is not aware they are an empath or is but doesn't know how to control it and as a result do not properly center their energy and emotions. A structured empath is one who knows they are an empath, properly grounds, and centers their energy and then is also able to maintain their personal energy space and use their empath abilities to their advantage and others. Most of us have been operating as unstructured empaths up to this point. As a result, we absorb instead of observing, which causes energetic imbalances that appear to manifest emotionally.

THREE STEPS IN YOUR ENERGY AND EMOTIONAL EVOLUTION:

1. Sitting in the discovery and acceptance that you are an empath
2. Working through centering your energy and getting aligned to zero-point
3. Learning to use your energy for protection, transmuting, shielding, and redirecting.

FOR AN INTUITIVE, TWO STEPS:

1. Sitting in the discovery and acceptance, you have extrasensory perception abilities
2. Learning to hone your talents and make them stronger

When I had initially discovered I was an empath, there was a period of me that sat in the space of just wanting to hold the small child I once was. Why are you so emotional? Because I am an empath … and never knew. Heck, even my mother had never heard of that term before.

ENERGY VAMPIRES

An energy vampire is someone who literally sucks your vibrational energy out of you and into a lower frequency vibration. I used to call these people Debbie Downers. They are people that you find yourself not enjoying their company in any capacity because of how you physically feel around them. If you are an empath, you need to identify who the energy vampires are that are in your life. From there, my advice is to simply just stay away from them. If you choose not to or can't because of work or family, you need to make sure you are actively centering and clearing your energy daily to deal with them.

EMPATHS AND NARCISSISTS

In researching more on empaths, I found that empaths go hand in hand with narcissists. I would say most people probably are familiar with the general Greek myth of Narcissus, who was a hunter known for his beauty. As a result, the term narcissist is often referred to someone who is fixated with their appearance and public perception of themself. However, that isn't actually what a narcissist is. Let's rephrase that definition for you.

Whether you want to say narcissist or the psychology definition of narcissistic personality disorder, either works. A narcissist is one who involves a pattern of self-centered, arrogant thinking and behavior. They lack empathy and consideration for other people and have an excessive need for admiration which could be based on their accomplishments. They are not necessarily the most beautiful people. They can also be described as manipulative, controlling, selfish, patronizing, and demanding.

The way they think and behave is prevalent in every area of the narcissist's life, from work and friendships to family and love relationships.

Narcissists are extremely resistant to changing their behavior, even when it's causing them problems. They have a tendency to redirect the blame on others. They react poorly to the slightest criticisms, disagreements, or perceived slights, which they view as personal attacks. They expect constant and undivided attention and admiration but aren't able to take others' needs and feelings into consideration. They are full of insults and condescension, but fly off the handle at the slightest bit of criticism toward them.

So why are narcissists attracted to empaths? Empaths are the opposite of narcissists. They are attracted to people they will get the greatest use from. Whereas narcissists have no empathy and thrive on the need for admiration, empaths are extremely sensitive, compassionate, and in tune with other people's emotions and want to help. Narcissists present a false self, where they appear charming and intelligent until you don't do things their way, and then they turn. Narcissists are psychologically intelligent, cunning, and manipulative in ways that an empath just doesn't process as behavior one should imbue. I suggest either reading up on the psychology of narcissists as well as empaths or consult a medical health professional if you realize you have been subjected to abuse from a narcissist.

At this point, if you hadn't connected it already, the narcissists are a soul contract you made or one that was made by two other associated spirits. If it was a soul contract you made, then both of you were meant to roll into each other's life to learn something. It might not be pleasant. It might not be what your current self is happy about. But this is the experience, and you agreed to it. So now you have to sit in that space of acceptance of that knowledge. Where you have to get to is how to handle this situation as a whole and what are the choices you are going to make with this shift in your perception. Do you feel more compassionate but understanding and realizing you have to sever that? Or do you feel compelled to approach it entirely differently, and maybe you are the one that heals you both?

If it was an encounter that was by association to one of your primary soul contracts, then if that person inflicts a violation against another light-based spirit such as you, it creates a karmic energy cord automatically, and it becomes a soul contract you never agreed to, but now are bound by the energetic situation. You can get rid of these energy entanglements, and I will explain later how to do so. Some people say that every major experience with someone is a contract you made, but I just don't believe that. We all have the element of choice, which means we are each essentially playing our own version of a chess game with other people. If everyone automatically made all these contracts ahead of time, then everything is preordained, and there is no such thing as choice or free will because everything is predictable.

Children raised in environments where they felt safe, secure, loved, and cared for are typically highly empathic. Many but not all empaths are that way due to trauma (emotional or physical), and that trauma doesn't just heal overnight. I highly recommend mental health therapy. Simply find someone that wants to talk it through. I had already been doing therapy for years as a way to work through my emotional pain, and we really should lean more into mental health treatment for anyone who needs it and wants it. The mind is a machine, and all machines need maintenance. Just make sure you find someone who you think you will be comfortable with. If you are currently in an abusive relationship, then you need to quietly work on a plan to resolve or escape and establish new boundaries.

To read up more on empaths and narcissists in greater detail, I suggest looking into the books by psychiatrist Judith Orloff, especially *The Empath's Survival's Guide*. If you were a child of a narcissistic parent or have been in a toxic relationship with a narcissist, I suggest you pick up a book to explore further the depth of that kind of relationship and how to recover from it. You will have a much greater understanding at the psychological level of the other person as well as yourself and your situations and why they have gone round and round. Now I ask you, can you identify the narcissists in your life, protect yourself from their power plays, and establish healthier boundaries?

CHAPTER 23

EMOTIONAL TRIGGERS
AND REDIRECTS

Whoever controls the mind controls the soul. So what emotionally controls you? Don't let the storm draw you in. You will feel tempted to engage. The redirecting process creates a shift in your timeline as you become less predictable in your decisions and choices. You will make improvements, and then the universe has a funny way of saying, but are you sure? Be sure again, and the time after that, and then it starts to all change. When you block or suppress emotions, it becomes a perpetual loop. The path to clearing karmic cycles deals with both your current life and ties to your future ones. Clearing karmic ties involves releasing energy that no longer suits your purpose, which raises your personal vibration or frequency level, and when that happens, it positively affects the collective consciousness.

If love creates or strengthens trust, then deception breaks it. Fear, anger, jealousy, and betrayal sabotage building the bonds of trust. People lie out of love, hate, fear, greed, or a sense of self-preservation. We may believe that we wouldn't do a particular thing to someone and are surprised when someone else does this to us. Think of all the trauma/betrayal faced in this lifetime. Now layer it with thousands of lifetimes but in worse time periods. When you realize that the conflicts you are having in this lifetime are simply a regurgitation of sorts of past lifetimes and experiences, it starts to make sense. The people you have conflict with, you have had it before. Maybe not exactly the same, but it's not the first rodeo between you and those souls.

Having ease within your life doesn't mean life will be easy to navigate. Instead, it is acting on decisions to not make your life more complicated. There are people in your life you made contracts with, and they came into your life for a reason. Then there are others by proximity you simply are around and have to deal with. We will discuss the latter first.

Emotional triggers are situations that occur that make you snap on a dime. Maybe that invokes tears, anger, disgust, confusion or some other negative feeling that takes you from being totally fine to darn near unhinged. When I examined the situations in my life that made me flip that switch, I then looked at the root cause of those situations. What I found is that I have two primary Achilles' heels. The first one I realized, most people also share this in common—> Deception. Any form of deception, lying especially but deception with the preplanned intent to deceive. Deception breaks the bonds of trust, honesty, and maybe loyalty pending the situation.

Most of the deception for me stems from the idea, how could you as a human being actively have the thought and intention that you are completely okay deceiving this person? Yet deception is the crux of this entire problem on Earth we have going on. We are deceived by the information we are spoon-fed by the media and corporations. We are deceived by what the government is really doing. We are deceived by our loved ones at different points in time for different reasons. We are deceived by our employers in a variety of ways as well. We also are deceived by our friends sometimes.

I also realized that I knew where 90% of all my emotional triggers would come from, which means I know who the individuals are that will trigger me before I ever have an event. That is important. Look at your situations and identify who the people are that are the consistent emotional triggers for you, and then look at the real root of that trigger. Is it because they refuse to acknowledge something? Is it simply their behavior and treatment toward you, and if so, why?

My second emotional trigger is ignorance embroiled in arrogance. The overwhelming majority of the time I am faced with this situation is in my professional occupation. I can navigate situations with any logical individual because we can speak the language of common sense. Even if that means I don't get my way, we navigate that landscape together to come up with a solution that usually involves some give and take. Quite simply, that is called teamwork. But when I am dealing with an individual at work in a position of power and authority who either fails or refuses to abide by data, facts, my knowledge, and experience and simply doesn't care, and they just want what they want because they want it or committed people to do it without any fundamental data to support it, that is where I get triggered.

To get myself out of that headspace, I realized I needed to change how I mentally operated with my emotional triggers with people I had to deal with. I call this—redirecting my emotional triggers.

+ Step 1: Identify what/where/who the majority of your emotional triggers come from.
+ Step 2: Know that they will occur again but don't sit in the worry of it.
+ Step 3: Know you are more intelligent and intuitive than the other person in question, and you will see the deception or ignorance.
+ Step 4: Be smarter and more strategic than they are in preparation for it.

In my work situation, the best decision would be to find a new job, one that would restore my sense of self-worth and bring me some level of joy or satisfaction. However, given that my job allowed certain flexibility in my personal situation along with some other positives, I chose to use my job situation as a way for me to work through my emotional triggers.

Every morning as I opened my laptop to start my day, I said, you know you will be faced with something today, and you know where it most likely will come from. Then like expected, something happened. In the beginning, I decided when this happened, instead of swearing at my laptop and spiking my frustration and anger, I chose to get up and walk away for several minutes. Then I would come back and refocus myself. After awhile, I got to the point where I didn't have to get up anymore. Instead, I would see the nonsense fly across my email or IM and ... I would read it, then ignore it for a bit.

Interestingly enough, when I held back, half the time, others stepped forward with their opinions first, which ended up making me not always look like the primary voice of opposition. By the time I would chime in, it was usually shorter than what I first would have written or said, and I was more or less supporting someone else. The point I got to after that was pretty much an eye roll when I saw the nonsense. When you are dealing with people who don't care about facts, nor are they giving you specific answers on how they are going to solve your problems, you have to find a place of peace within the madness of that. However, this job will become hazardous to my health, and I have a plan in place to do something else as a transition.

Figure out how you can restructure a relationship you currently have. Maybe with a parent, a sibling, a friend, or your partner. You may choose to completely remove someone from your life due to their toxicity. That is okay as you are simply maintaining your boundaries and your energy field to be at a higher vibration. Lots of people do. They cut off their family if that is what is needed for their best version of their higher self. I have done it myself. Some of these contracts are to force you to get rid of the negativity. Some may be to push you into something new and to what you are meant to. Life has a way of forcing the issue if you are not on the right path. Your spirit guides are part of that. Trying to create havoc to force you to go in a different direction, the one in which you belong according to your blueprint.

When you think of the people in question, you need to view them differently. I now look at people as low vibrational vs high vibrational and intelligent or not. When you realize the type of person you are dealing with, it starts to change how you operate with them. In my example of work, I realize I am dealing with someone who is middle to low vibration and is unintelligent. This is pretty much a no-win battle. So the only thing I can do is realize I am dealing with that kind of person. Then I simply use facts in my information. It doesn't matter if my facts are ignored as they will be. What matters is that I put the facts out there, repeatedly and if this ever goes to a manager outside the project, then as long as they aren't unintelligent, they will see what is happening and say. At a minimum, you are holding yourself to a level of integrity, and that is most important.

Part of healing yourself is learning to love yourself. To change your own view of yourself and to eliminate the negative programming you have been subjected to in this lifetime. I am a believer of healing yourself first in this lifetime, then heal your previous lifetimes, and then once you have done that, then you can choose to work with healing others. If you try to heal others before you have healed yourself, then you bring any negative ties holding on to you in their energy space.

Here is an exercise I did when looking at how to learn to love myself more than simply saying, screw everyone, I'm good how I am. That isn't the love I am speaking of here. This kind of love is a combination of acceptance of yourself and forgiveness of your role in the grand scheme of things. In my past, my predominate view of myself was this:

Too headstrong, too controlling, too emotionally unbalanced, mean/rude, a bulldozer, sad and upset, constantly let down by others, bitchy, impatient, confused, weak/low self-esteem and self-image, piss poor attitude at times, too trusting when I should not have been and not trusting when I should, aggressive, low-value system, not believing I am smart or good enough, I say yes too much, cuts people off when talking. That's a pretty poor self-evaluation of myself, wouldn't you say?

This list was one of the first things I wrote during my journey and circling back to now when I am formally reviewing it again, but from the other side, I felt pain reading it. Knowing my self-worth for years was centered around the concept of: I have no value, and I am not special. Sitting in the knowledge that I do, in fact, have value, and in a position of loving myself, it makes me cry with so much compassion for my past self that it physically hurts. At the same time, there is also a certain irony in that list.

Example: too headstrong. The reason I am so headstrong is because of the injustices I have faced at all points in my life and the complete refusal to be reduced to a minuscule contributor. As a woman, I have been discounted, belittled, underestimated, ignored, diminished, talked down to when the men above me just "don't like what I say" because it was truth that pointed out problems/risks in a situation or their personal flaws that are contributing to the failure of something versus the success of it.

Most men do not like strong, outspoken women. They believe women have a place, and that place does not dwell in equality in any capacity. There are men that lean into this except when it comes to their woman and social situations, exuding the illusion publicly as if they are allies to women when they aren't. Don't get me wrong, not all men are like this, and I am not a man-hater. Men have wonderful attributes that complement female attributes, and there are many men that both understand this and are also allies of women in our quest to be treated fairly and equally and without prejudice or as an object solely for the purpose of a man's desire.

After writing this list, I said, now who do I want to be in the future? Or how do I want to view myself moving forward? So I wrote a new list of attributes I wanted to identify with: Brave, strong, nice, positive, thoughtful, loving, protective, nurturing, loyal, friendly, observant, passionate, compassionate, determined, intelligent, independent, empathic, better manners in communication, and knowledgeable.

The irony with my future list is that all but five are traits I possessed when I made out the first list. Part of this is how you choose to view yourself vs the projection others have placed on you. It actually took friends and some family over the years telling me I was a thoughtful person about things I do for them for me to even consider myself as a thoughtful person. The thoughts you have toward yourself are powerful. They create a loop in your mind and form consistent patterns. In order to get out of those patterns, you have to think differently. It is tricky but to change your scripts is to change your perception of yourself. This is where the term "self-love" or "loving yourself" comes in to play. Instead of focusing on all the things you wish you would or could change about yourself, you have to instead start looking at and quantifying the good qualities you have.

One helpful way to do this is to have a morning and or nightly affirmation. When you wake up, take a minute to remind yourself about the awesome person you are and how you are going to have a positive day, and the strength to deal with anything that comes your way. You can do the same at night and even list out the things you are grateful for or the lessons you learned that day. By rewiring yourself to have these positive affirmations about yourself, you start to rewire the neurons in your brain to function differently. This is the true power of the mind.

Do you have a parent or a sibling or some other very close individual in your life who has a shared history but has opposing views of that event, and your version is not positive? Every time you find yourself around this person, there is still some underlying respite. And you are really mad about it. You want them to validate your version of reality. This is where your throat chakra gets locked, and dis-ease begins, usually targeting the thyroid or jaw.

You first have to sit in the knowledge that your reality is your truth. It may not be *the* truth. It is your truth. Accept that it doesn't matter who agrees with you or not, you know what your truth is. When you are able to come to closure on that, listen to meditation music for unlocking your throat chakra. You will also want to say some mantras around coming to terms with this issue with this other person but from a calm perspective of greater clarity. That you no longer want to give energy to this issue, and it doesn't serve any further purpose for you in this life. Send the other person loving energy so that maybe it opens a space in their heart or mind. At any rate, this is compassion and forgiveness in a situation. Understand that some people are not capable of dealing with the emotional impacts that come with understanding another person's version of events.

In other situations where someone comes on very negative or strong, you need to see that it really is a mirror for the aggressor. It is rooted in that person's insecurities, weaknesses, blind spots. While it feels very personal, it is simply their pain and frustration lashing out. This is where you start going from ready to engage with that person defiantly, to one of wait, I recognize what is really going on here, then centering your mind, grounding your etheric energy, and instead start feeling compassion for them.

Your responses become less reactionary, more controlled, and calmer. You are seeing the situation for what it really is, instead of the surface layer impression. They can't see what they need to work on and heal, and might never. It can be difficult once you get on this side of changing your scripts and dealing with people, because you wish they saw things in this newer light of clarity too. It would help everyone if they did.

We all have at least one or several people in our lives we have strong energetic connections to that we also have conflicts with. One of which for me was my mother. I was in a unique situation with her and this process of my Awakening, because she had died a year and a half before. Being adopted, aside from when it was revealed I was adopted, I always had a connection with my mother. I always looked up to her for her strength, mental resolve in the face of heavy conflict. I was crushed when she was crushed, yet sad when she was happy because it meant she was hopped up on a lot of prescription medication. A lot of us have a complicated mother or father story.

When you become a parent yourself, you do a lot of looking back at your own childhood. How your parents handled situations, what the situations were, and how you are handling them in comparison. You have a few situations that innately change once you have a child. Where you think, "Wow, I think mom and dad missed the boat on that one, and that is an area we will be doing differently with our child." Having a child myself, there isn't anything I wouldn't do for him, and I am actually extra protective of him and his emotional and mental stability as it relates to anyone that comes into my life.

If there was a situation where a man crossed a line with me over my son, that is it, get the fuck out. This is my spawn. Men may come and go, but this is my spawn. So anything outside of that seems foreign to me. I take the responsibility of keeping him safe from predators of all kinds seriously, and educate him on the evils in life. As a mother, I don't want to be hearing a story twenty years later of something that happened on my watch that I either could have prevented or should have been more diligent about. When I look at my mother's choice from that as a parent, I am saddened she didn't feel that way.

I grew up not being taught proper conflict negotiation. It caused problems in a lot of my early relationships and has been something I have had to work on for a long time to get to a mature place. It took having another person being mature in that arena, to say, I will hold this space for you, and when you are ready to be calm, we can talk.

Being raised Catholic, you just understood that marriage wasn't always easy, it was a lot of hard work, but you have to stay in it. This was a conflict for me that took a long time to work through over the years. At what point does common sense trump loyalty? At what point is the line between commitment no matter what changed to respecting yourself to no longer be violated? Hate the sin, love the sinner. What is the line on that really though? Love the man that hits you, not the fact that he did hit you. Love the man with violent alcohol addiction issues, not that he has alcoholism, and because he only acts out once a week. Over time though, I started to realize my mother's religion was keeping her in her situation and it was not the right answer.

I had come to a place years before in therapy where I had to grieve the fact I did not get to have the mother I needed or wanted. That I needed to identify what the best possible relationship with her looked like, and then simply cater to that. For me, it was a death of my mother during that time. From her perspective our relationship improved. From mine, it was a facade. One held due to the innate ties I felt to her. But it wasn't a relationship I was willing to sever. It was one I always wished she would change, but she didn't. I couldn't even have a private conversation with her as an adult, so most of my conversations ended up being surface stuff. When I was in college, she picked up the phone and called me a total of four times in four years. That was it. When I called, if it had been awhile, she would say, well, I hadn't heard from you in a while. I wanted to say, "You know the phone works both ways, right?"

When she died, I expected to get some of her ashes per the direction we had been given a few years ago on their end-of-life wishes. That didn't happen, and apparently, there was a new direction that indicated I would never get them. The entire situation around her death being a little suspicious as well. I had to get to a place of letting it all go. I had to let her go in all its capacity. It was hard to do and didn't happen overnight.

During my Awakening, I discovered that she actually had an idea of what was happening to me as a child. But she couldn't prove it, and I don't know if she ever tried. But the fact there was suspicion, and she had been confronted on it, and had refused to even take it remotely seriously, was a new layer of damage and shadow work I had to contend with. I had to grieve the notion that my mother failed to protect me after she had been confronted by another family member. A family member who wasn't even around me day to day could tell something was wrong, but as a mother, she completely failed to read the signs that her daughter was going through some form of emotional and mental trauma, not to mention physically. "What is wrong with you? Why are you so emotional?" I had to forgive and let this go too.

When dealing with someone who is deceased, they still have a spirit. Even if they have reincarnated, their spirit still has a connection to Source, and you are connected to Source, so you can still heal this. In some ways, I almost think it was easier to heal this issue with my mother being that she was deceased than if I had to confront her when she was alive and deal with it that way. Whereas she could never buy into the notion that my brother or I had been victims in our youth, I was able to see that she had been just as much a victim. It wasn't even about who was the bigger victim that did not matter. What mattered is *all* the victims healed and turned into survivors.

When I called her spirit into my presence for the letting go moment, she, of course, having more access to the knowledge of her life in etheric form than when she was in it, already knew the horror. It was an intense feeling I got with her, that while I was willing to forgive her on this topic, that she wasn't willing to forgive herself for the role she played. It was a very emotional fifteen minutes for me to verbally reconcile this with her and change our energy and mental dynamics.

When you look back at your situations and relationships, were there personal boundaries that were crossed? If so, then try to look at them from more of a vanilla idea that these were just soul contracts meant for you to have an experience and learn something on Earth. We aren't meant to just be born, work as slaves, die, and do it all over again. That is what has been happening, but that isn't what is supposed to be happening. When you are ready to let these people go, spend some time writing a letter about everything you feel. When you are ready, read it out loud, cry if you have to, release any anger or hatred, resentment, or blame you had been holding on to. Send them loving energy telepathically and burn the letter. State to yourself that you are ready to release all of the negativity you have been holding on to as it no longer serves a purpose. It is to vacate your physical and etheric layers, and in its place, you wish to usher in peace, compassion, and understanding.

Each primary emotion resonates at a specific frequency. Joy is the highest, then love. Anger, hate, guilt, and shame resonate the lowest. Healing occurs when you let the negativity go. This is how you change the vibrational frequency of your body, your soul, and even your mind.

At some point, you will come to terms with the fact that some people, while part of your history, aren't meant to be part of your destiny and that their part in your story is over. Once you realize who those are, you can start to let go of past situations.

CHAPTER 24

CHAKRAS

WHAT IS A CHAKRA?

Chakra means "wheel" and refers to energy points in your body. They are illustrated as spinning disks of energy that correspond to nerves, organs, and all areas of our energetic body that affect our emotional and physical well-being.

Every person has an aura, which simply is an electromagnetic energy field that surrounds people (and animals). You also have a toroidal field that intertwines the etheric soul with the physical body and reverberates from the heart chakra. Your aura automatically connects to the ethereal plane in order to record this data via energy pathways (Akashic Records).

This energy source I just described above is all energy simply moving and operating at different frequencies in various vibrational synchronicity with each other. As does the body but in a denser matter way.

If you think this is odd, think for a moment that there are things you know exist, but you can't see. You can't see the music that comes out of a radio, yet you know it exists, because one of your senses engages with the vibrational output that light and sound produces. You know that microwaves magically cook your food even though you can't see how it actually works. It channels heat energy directly to heat molecules inside the food. You know energy exists, but only because you can see the outcome that it produces. You also know that with every major discovery, that previously, it was something that was considered as ... nonexistent or not real because they simply couldn't prove it using the technological methods and information collected and reviewed available at that time.

There are seven primary layers of your aura that correspond with the seven main chakras in the body.

1. Etheric layer (physical aura plane), which is closest to the physical body and is connected to physical health, pain, and pleasure.
2. Emotional layer (astral aura plane) that extends up to three inches away from the body.
3. Mental layer, which correlates to your solar plexus chakra which sits three to eight inches away and is related to your ego, values, and beliefs.
4. Astral layer (love plane). It connects to the heart chakra and sits right in the middle of all seven main energy chakras, so it's said to connect the three lower auric planes to the three higher ones.
5. Manifestation layer connects to your throat chakra, the spiritual aura plane. It reflects your spiritual health and connects you to the wider universe.

6. Celestial plane, which is all about your intuition and is linked with your third eye chakra.
7. Ketheric layer that connects to your seventh chakra of mind and consciousness ... this is your potential connection with the Divine/Source. It extends up to three feet away from the physical body.

Each chakra is associated with a color that reflects a type of vibrational frequency. Each color represents something as well, and healing crystals are also associated with each chakra. Your seven primary chakras are as follows:

ROOT CHAKRA

+ Trust Chakra and deals with survival and is blocked by fear
+ Red (Color) identifies with safety, survival, grounding, and nourishment from Earth energy
+ Red can also indicate inflammation at a physical level
+ Healing Crystals = Agate, Black Tourmaline, Hematite, Tiger's Eye

SACRAL CHAKRA

+ Sexual energy deals with sexuality/creativity and is blocked by guilt
+ Orange (Color) identifies with emotions, creativity, sexuality, and is associated with water and flow
+ Healing Crystals = Citrine, Coral, Moonstone

SOLAR PLEXUS CHAKRA

+ Power deals with wisdom/power and is blocked by shame
+ Yellow (Color) = mental activities, intellect, personal power, and will
+ Healing Crystals = Orange Calcite, Citrine, Malachite, Topaz

HEART CHAKRA
+ Love deals with love/healing and is blocked by grief
+ Green (Color) = love, relating, integration, compassion
+ Healing Crystals = Green Calcite, Green Tourmaline, Jade, Rose Quartz

THROAT CHAKRA
+ Communication) deals with truth and is blocked by lies
+ Blue (Color) = self-expression, expression of truth, creative expression, communication, perfect form, and patterns
+ Healing Crystals = Aquamarine, Lapis Lazuli, Turquoise

THIRD EYE CHAKRA
+ Intuition deals with insight/awareness and is blocked by illusion
+ Purple (Color) = intuition, extrasensory perception, inner wisdom
+ Healing Crystals = Amethyst, Black Obsidian, Purple Fluorite

CROWN CHAKRA
+ Head deals with pure cosmic energy/spirituality and is blocked by Earthly attachment
+ White (Color) = association with the universe, connection with spirituality and consciousness
+ Healing Crystals = Amethyst, Diamond, Clear Quartz, Selenite

If you have a child, and when they were young, were there moments you looked at them and just knew what they needed or wanted? Same thing. Using psychic intuition to make a determination. Same for a significant other? Your chakras are energetically aligned. Of course, you understand when there is an energetic disturbance. That moment you know there is a problem, but the other person won't admit it. Only for time to go by, and then they admit what they've been thinking or feeling? Meanwhile, you are sitting there saying to yourself, "I KNEW IT." That is an example of energy transference and your higher consciousness psychic interpretation of what it received.

From chakras, we leap to Kundalini energy. Kundalini energy is a form of energy and consciousness located at the base of the spine. Your level of consciousness depends on the direction the energy takes. When your dormant Kundalini flows freely up through the seven chakras, it is known as a Kundalini Awakening. This energy helps bring you to a place of energetically dissolving your self-identification, beliefs, and illusions you have been operating under your entire life. Some people say it feels like a snake actually uncoiling and an energetic zipping up the spine all the way to the crown chakra.

The chakras are important for many reasons. This is ancient eastern medicine knowledge that has been around for thousands of years. When you have a trauma, death of a loved one, near-death experience, abuse, neglect, addiction, or anything that you personally identify with as a trauma in your life, then your chakras effectively get hijacked on the energy flow within you. If there is an irritant to it, then the chakras that correspond to those emotional centers associated with the trauma will start to send out damaging signals to a nearby area in the body.

To take that one step further, you have both physical and etheric matching DNA markers for dis-eases. Those DNA' markers were put in place as part of your blueprint, knowing you would have this type of experience at some point in your life, and if you weren't able to easily move past it, then signals would send out and activate the physical DNA markers that are mirrored in your etheric layer. All the DNA from all the lifetimes you have had is encoded in your light-based spirit of consciousness. Think of it like your spirit being a light-based mathematical computation that contains all of these complex algorithms that were all mapped to different density experiences but still encoded in the essence of you.

In order to clear your chakras, meditation music is super helpful. Sometimes it just makes you feel good or calm. Sometimes I have cried. I made the mistake the first time I found myself crying, I shut it off. My brain processed that I was crying as a negative thing, and that I needed to stop the negative thing. But what I needed was to finish out that session and let whatever emotion needed to be expelled to come out. Otherwise, I was resisting the very thing that was trying to help me.

Reiki is another solution for getting your chakras unlocked. Understand that a really good healer can heal you no matter where they are on the planet, because energy has no bounds through time and space. However, there are many people who are just starting the healing processes, so be kind to them in their own learning and growth.

You can also do a visualization exercise of unlocking your chakras by imaging you are turning a wheel or a round lock, and you are unlocking it with your entire hand. If you have thyroid issues, then you have to clear your trauma on what truth it is that is being blocked by someone else. You need to either resolve the relationship or you need to resolve the conflict in yourself. It might mean you stand firmly in your truth, but you stop trying to have the other person validate your position. That is effectively … letting go.

Why is this important? Because in order for you to physically feel better, you have to release the negative emotions weighing you down, which are cycling through your chakras. By releasing the negative energy and aligning yourself—mind, body, and spirit—your body can start to self-heal. The mind is a powerful thing. When energy is flowing through the brain, and your consciousness is operating in a calmer zone, then your brain sends signals to the cells in your body to start repairing themselves. This is the science of psychology. There is a lot more information available in other books and sites regarding chakras should you choose to research further.

Every individual has feminine and masculine energy. This is represented with the Yin and Yang symbol showing the duality and yet how that duality is actually a unity of one in balance and harmony to form polarity. The question simply is, do you have more of one quality than the other, or do you sit in balance with both energies—embracing the beautiful aspects that they each bring and combine within your spirit?

Masculine energy is associated with the ego. The predominant qualities that make up the masculine energy are logic, survival, reason, leadership, action, and strength. Feminine energy is associated with nurturing. The predominant qualities that feminine energy possess are intuition, healing, wisdom, patience, and emotions. In our reality on Earth, we see these as separate from each other instead of working in tandem, and as a result, we try to tie them directly into gender. But that is a flawed concept. I am a woman that has had more masculine energy in my lifetime mixed with a lower dose of feminine energy. The imbalance in my feminine energy is what I have had to repair during my Awakening. However, I am a heterosexual female. Are you starting to see how gender does not implicate masculine or feminine energy?

CHAPTER 25

CRYSTALS

s a child, I loved rocks of all sorts. I would collect them, look at them, play with them, a lot of which was quartz. I did this until I realized that it wasn't cool for girls to play with rocks or have a rock collection. When I discovered I was an empath, I also was led to crystals. At the time, I remember thinking, oh no, I don't want to become one of those people. You know the hippie crystal people. But as I looked into crystals and the science behind them, I was surprised at what I found.

Crystals are actually stones that each vibrate at a different frequency. I wasn't quite at the understanding of frequencies just yet, or how crystals really worked, but I had someone tell me, "You know that's why there are quartz crystals in watches right? Because they hold a consistent frequency as energy travels through them, which remains constant because they are not organic matter. Which also means, they reverberate back to the receiver the frequency they carry, which in turn, will change the frequency of a bio-electrical being (aka a human)."

Crystals are found in cell phones, the first radios, satellites, and much more. Another interesting component of crystals is that digital data can be stored in quartz crystals. In fact, we can store more data in a crystal smaller than a BB than we can in an entire thumb drive. Quartz crystal technology for storing data is used in just about every electrical technology we possess today, from phones to satellites. In the late 1800s, crystal skulls were found in South America. The origins of these skulls are a mystery to archeologists, as well as what their function is. The skulls do not contain any tool marks whatsoever, and it is wondered if ancient technology is stored in the skulls, but we just aren't smart enough to figure it out.

On the healing side, different crystals have been found to amplify different things. Rose quartz is a calming crystal, whereas amethyst is associated with enhancing the third eye chakra. Common crystals are selenite, rose quartz, sodalite, jasper, citrine, moonstone, aquamarine, obsidian, aventurine, hematite, tiger's eye, labradorite, fluorite, agate and many more. Because the information on healing crystals is so abundant between books and what is found on the internet, I have chosen not to do an in-depth review of crystals and instead simply encourage you to seek out your own research on them. There is a plethora of good information out there for you to read.

What I will tell you is this. When choosing crystals, beyond what they represent, it is important that you choose crystals that you are personally drawn to. If you are drawn specifically to some more than others, then that is part of your calling card, and those are the ones you need to get. I like to have obsidian in my house as protection against negative energy, among other stones. Rose quartz and selenite are both crystals that calm my energy into a synthesis. I remember buying this five-inch selenite crystal and just holding it. After five minutes, that massive current of energy, I always felt, started to go away. I felt energetically calm, which was both weird, surprising, and also enlightening. I had just found an easy trick to change my own energy frequency to one of more balance, all through a rock.

I finally understood something else. Anytime I had done public speaking, I would shake. I thought maybe it was nerves, but it always felt like something else. I would know the content, the audience was friendly, and if you knew me, you would think—definitely a great public speaker. But I hated it. The moment I would be in front of everyone, I would get goosebumps on my legs that would stay, my stomach would start flipping in summersaults, I would start shaking, and then my throat would start to reverberate as I was speaking so you could hear the waver in my voice. What I now understand in my research as an empath is that we draw energy to us from others. So when I would stand up in front of a room of people as a natural, high-energy transmitter and receiver. I was getting every person's energy targeted directly on me, and it would energetically set me off balance. It would reverberate my chakra main line up to my throat, and that was the waver in my throat.

Before this, the only way I could try not to have a total meltdown was to look at the audience, pick out three to four friendly faces spread out in the room, and then as I would speak, I would jump my eyes from one friendly face to the other by scanning the crowd slowly enough to make it look like I was focusing on others as I talked but would move fast enough to the next person, that the crowd couldn't tell. It was the only way to hold on to the iota of sanity in those moments.

When I feel a little off in my solar plexus or right above it, I wear a quartz crystal necklace to calm me down. Sometimes I put a couple of small stones in my bra between my boobs. Works in minutes. I've also used them for cramps and bulging discs. You can place them in your space, hold them, put a couple in your pockets, make interesting design formations with them. Whatever you come up with, is totally fine. Another element that is fun to work with is crystal designs using sacred geometry. There are several books available on this topic as well. There is no wrong way to work with crystals.

In reviewing hematite properties, I had a new understanding of that one as well. As someone who has always had high energy, I have always been drawn to hematite like a fly to a zapper. Hematite is a grounding stone. Through my teens and early adulthood, I would often see a hematite bracelet, necklace, or ring and feel as if I had to have it. I just thought it was because I liked the shiny color. But my body was saying—yeah, this one is good for you because of the energy you contain.

Epsom salt is interesting for its healing properties in removing toxins from the body. Epsom salt is actually a combination of magnesium and sulfate. When magnesium sulfate is absorbed through the skin, it draws toxins from the body, sedates the nervous system, reduces swelling, relaxes muscles, and more.

Salt lamps claim they can clean the air in your home, soothe allergies, boost your mood, and help you sleep. Salt lamps are natural ionizers, meaning they change the electrical charge of the circulating air. Ions are compounds that carry a charge because they have an unbalanced number of protons or electrons. They are produced naturally in the air when alterations occur in the atmosphere. Himalayan salt lamps produce ions by attracting water particles that evaporate off as a salt solution when heated by the lamp, forming mostly negative ions.

If you are an empath then it is critical that you have crystals in your space or on you. Ever since I have added crystals into my mine, I no longer get shocked twenty times a day on everything, which used to be a normal occurrence in my life. Make sure that you clear the energy on them frequently. To do so, there is sunlight, moonlight, and some natural stones that can be cleaned with running water and energy mantras. Just make sure you check to see what crystals can be subjected to water, because not all can.

So my lifecycle with crystals went from, I love them as a child to … they are not cool to … oh, no I don't want to be a crystal chick … to crystals work in weird ways … how can I get more.

CHAPTER 26

MEDITATION, GROUNDING, CENTERING, AND SHIELDING YOUR ENERGY

For me, being an empath meant I was all over the map emotionally and energetically until I started doing various forms of grounding and meditation. Meditation is a practice many thousands of years old and done all around the world.

If you are not someone who practices meditation currently, then let me give you a rundown. First of all, meditation is a very personal thing. It is something to do daily, and it is the key component of you learning to look within yourself for the answers and as a way to calm yourself to an energetically centered state. Meditation alters your brain waves to vibrate at a different frequency, thereby allowing other insights to occur.

ACTIVE MEDITATION

Active Meditation is different from traditional meditation because you are active. Some people might find going for miles on end running is their way of doing active meditation. Or cleaning your house. A time when they can focus on themselves without external distractions and at the same time, energetically get your mind to match your physical body. For some people who constantly hear their spirit guides, this can be a reprieve from the constant chatter you hear as you can zone out into some physical activity, and that allows you to quiet your mind. I personally do both because I have an active mind, so this helps me get my thoughts out; at the same time, I also need to quiet it.

PASSIVE MEDITATION

I call traditional meditation passive meditation as it is designed to change your frequency and put your brain waves into a different frequency state through inner reflection. Passive meditation is where you might be silent and visualize. Maybe you speak to your guides. Maybe you have candles and crystals or singing bowls. Your path in meditation is up to you.

When I first tried meditation, I would get an immediate headache cramp on my crown chakra. As a result, I stumbled upon a technique that made it easier for me to go in. It is a counting technique where you count with your eyes closed for five to ten seconds, then open your eyes and look straight ahead at something. Close your eyes again and repeat up to twenty. Repeat again up to thirty or until you drop off. If visualizing is a challenge, like if you just see black space, then you need to trigger visualization.

Imagine in the black space that there is a door in the distance—just a plain door with a doorknob. Before you go to the door, think about a place you want to be when you enter the door. Maybe it is a small pool with a waterfall, maybe it is an Asian temple, maybe it is a deserted island, or somewhere you make up in your mind with fairies or something. When you open the door and walk through, visualize that place. If you are struggling still, try building the scene from your peripheral viewpoint and bridge it together in the middle. If this is hard, keep trying your meditation, and soon you will get there. Imagine you are smelling the scene and can touch the vegetation. Visualize every detail you can. Over time it gets easy, and your visualization processes speed up.

GROUNDING

I kept reading that I needed to ground and center my energy. But I didn't really know what that meant. In fact, everything I was reading made it seem like it was mentally grounding and centering my energy. I literally went months searching for this answer and kept looping into the same answers—go within to center yourself, or go be in nature. What does that really mean though? Can I be in nature at the park playing a game? Does that count? When I go within, what am I actually grounding? I kept searching because I still felt like I was missing something.

With the indication of being outside as a way to ground, I went looking for clearer answers among the vagueness. Then I stumbled upon the video The Science of Grounding by Clint Ober on YouTube. It was after watching that, my aha moment came flooding in. Physical grounding your energy is done when you are outside and touching the ground with no interference. I already discussed that the Earth has a toroidal field and humans have a toroidal field as well. When you pair your toroidal field with that of Earth's, it becomes a symbiotic balance of healing the Earth and yourself.

Electrons are in mass supply on the surface of the Earth, and when you realize that the root of all dis-ease is inflammation of cells, and that a damaged cell has had its electrons ejected, then grounding to the Earth as transmitters and receivers of energy, we absorb the electrons back into our body, and they reinsert themselves into the damaged cells, which begins natural healing. Toxins are also pulled down, and your meridians start to be in flow with the Earth's field. Ever wonder why most indigenous tribes don't have the dis-eases eastern culture does? One reason is that they still ground to the Earth daily just by their natural way of being.

As a collective consciousness, when we ground to the Earth (also called Earthing), we align our energy grids with that of Earth's and have the ability to raise the frequency we are all vibrating at. Physical grounding changes our vibrational frequency. It aligns the alpha waves in the brain, which are associated with deep relaxation. It is one thing to be physically present in nature—it is another to physically ground. You can touch the Earth with your feet, your hands, sitting, laying. You can do it with a blanket, but you cannot properly ground if you have something that is an insulator, such as rubber-soled shoes.

If you stand outside and think you are grounding in your tennis shoes, you aren't. Ever wonder how you can go to the beach and lie on hot lumpy sand, which is essentially concrete and get up just fine an hour later? That would be the electrons you are absorbing from the surface of the Earth. I highly recommend watching the Science of Grounding video. Medical studies were done and proven in all of them the scientific benefits in healing dis-eases and inflammation all through grounding. This is one of the areas if you currently have a dis-ease, immediately start doing this, even if it is five minutes here and five minutes there, or fifteen minutes a day. Whatever you can do, maybe it is being barefoot while sitting in a chair outside with your feet touching the Earth. Pavement or concrete? Not a conductor, but instead an insulator.

Doing grounding has been one of the single most contributors to healing my body from the damage of dis-ease. However, if you are like me, you might also be thinking, what about in winter, and I don't live at the beach? I'm not about to go outside in the freezing cold standing on the ground. It's a bit counterproductive. I figured, if Clint Ober figured out all this because he had an understanding of cable grounding and had consulted with doctors, maybe he had already figured out a solution. Turns out, he did. He came up with a grounding mat that you can put on your bed. It is very thin, has holes for breathability and safely conducts electron particles to the matt, which you absorb. While I personally noticed a stronger influence grounding with the Earth, the mat allowed me to effectively ground for six to eight hours at night, and I can tell you that made my body's healing process speed up dramatically.

CENTERING/SHIELDING YOUR ENERGY FIELD

Centering your energy is both a mental and energetic process. Think back to all the people whose energy you intertwined with today. Now in the last week, month, year. That's a lot! If you are an empath, then you have absorbed a lot of other people's energy, and they have grabbed some of yours. The first thing you need to do is get into a routine of daily clearing your energy field. In doing so, you also center your energy and clear your toroidal field and aura.

Start by sitting or standing somewhere quiet with your eyes closed. Focus on your breathing and take several deep breaths and exhale slowly.

Do this until your breathing naturally slows. Once you have pulled your-self down to a calm state, envision a ball of light. You can start with it above your head, or right in front of your solar plexus chakra. This ball of pure energy light should be a white or light golden color. If you envision from your solar plexus, then you want to visualize this ball of clean energy growing in size, all the way until your entire body is encapsulated in this ball of glowing light. If envisioning a ball of light from above, then the light grows in size from the top of your head all the way to below your root chakra and your feet. Envision this ball of energy and stand in the warmth and purity of it for several seconds. At this point, you need to verbally release and reclaim energy.

Release all energy in my energy field that has no purpose and return it back to the recipient it belongs to. I send it with love and peace. For anyone who has my energy intertwined in their fields that has no signifi-cant purpose, I reclaim my energy from them, clear it and bring it back to integrate with my energy field. I close all negative telepathic connections between anyone so as not to create further negative emotional cycles with them. I require all toxic energy in my space to be removed and transmuted into positive energy and send it down to the Earth to heal her. My shield is strong, and I add a layer of positive protection for myself as I encounter the situations of my day.

What you eventually will get to over time is being able to stand, envi-sion, and clear in less than a minute. Understand, you can alter statements to be more in line with wording that makes sense to you. You just need the framework and go from there. If you have problems visualizing the ball of light, here are some tips.

GROWING FROM YOUR SOLAR PLEXUS

Sometimes it is easier to start from within and move outward. In order to do so, imagine your solar plexus as an EMP that pulses out a signal through that ball of light. Each time, the EMP makes the ball of light bigger until eventually you are surrounded and hold it at that size.

Ball of light from top down.

If you struggle to get the ball or glow going, try these things. You have to work on your visualization then once you have it, you can learn to alter it much easier. Imagine instead you are being showered with raindrops of this energy from above. Some people even start out being in the shower and doing it and allowing the water to help with the visualization of the energy. You can also visualize glitter raining down, and eventually morphing the glitter into a sparkling ball of light. You can also visualize a waterfall of light blue or green silvery energy that flows to your head but instead spreads out, covering what was a round energy ball you just couldn't see.

You will find after doing this consistently that the next level up will be to hold your shield while in public. When you are ready for that, then use the solar plexus idea above and the EMP concept to help hold and maintain your energy shield while in an emotionally offsetting encounter with one or several people.

CHAPTER 27

SOUND THERAPY AND FREQUENCIES

Of the five primary senses we have, taste, touch, smell, sight, and hearing, only two of those senses are the ones we primarily rely on for our cognitive thinking and processing. We rely on our sight to tell us something we perceive is real. We rely on sound to help us process external factors that may be recorded without seeing. Taste, touch, and smell, on the other hand, are senses that only work in extreme close proximity, whereas sound and seeing is something we don't need to have in our personal space to experience.

Remember when I discussed in the Energy Chapter that all matter vibrates at a certain frequency? Your aura is your unique electromagnetic energy field that gives off vibrations. Your heart and brain process their functions through electrical stimuli and pulses.

The science of sound is an interesting one. Pythagoras was the first one to correlate that sound has frequencies. Different musical notes then vibrate at different frequencies, which we then perceive through our vestibulocochlear nerve (which transmits sound) and communicates balance to the brain. An opera singer whose voice can break glass is due to when acoustic sounds match kinetic energy vibrations, and it has an impact on that physical object.

It is important to note that people can be manipulated through sound frequencies, positively or negatively. Sound frequencies are also used to retrain brain waves to operate at a certain frequency, thereby retiring neuron patterns into a state where they are naturally wired to heal the body.

Human emotions have been mapped to resonate at different frequencies. Whereas love and joy have frequency levels on the high end, anger, fear, and shame are on the very low end. Those frequencies have a significant impact on your own frequency all the way down at the cellular level, which impacts the body's physical health. The emotional baggage you carry with you is what defines the personal frequency you resonate at. Sounds also are mapped to different frequencies, and sound therapy has been found to be an effective form of engaging the body to self-heal and align your chakras (energy centers) properly.

When you get to the point that you see people in terms of low vibrational vs high vibrational instead of assholes and nice people, your perception will start to shift, and how you respond to these types of people shift. To add further to the vibrational level there is high knowledge and low knowledge. When you find yourself in a situation where someone seems emotionally out of control and in your space, then they are operating at a low vibrational frequency (just with a lot of energy behind it). When you realize you are dealing with a low vibrational low intelligence person, you learn to feel a little more compassion for them. This is someone not capable of intelligent thought and not capable of getting their low vibrational energy elevated. High knowledge but low vibrational people though, those are the scary ones. Those are the people that you need to be careful of. They are intelligent but intentionally resonate at a low level of frequency … and they have for many lifetimes concurrently.

This is why meditation is important, because it allows you to put yourself into a different frequency which triggers the body to start self-healing. The specific sounds for healing, center around a tonal sound that vibrates at a certain harmonic frequency. The basic premise is that by listening to specific sound frequencies, your brain waves operate at different frequency levels, which the cells then send signals to the areas of the body to repair itself. There are different types of sound therapy.

AUDIO MUSIC

I personally like overnight sound therapy sessions, but you can listen to them while taking a salt bath or when meditating. I recommend these channels on YouTube:

+ Meditative Mind
+ Cleanse Aura
+ PowerThoughts Meditation Club
+ NRG8
+ Meditation and Healing

SINGING BOWLS

Singing bowls are rooted in sound therapy and also assist with putting your brain waves into a different frequency. Whether you want to use the singing bowls yourself, or you can find individuals on YouTube who do singing bowl meditations for you to simply listen to. Some sound therapy with singing bowls has the bowls placed on the individual, and the reverberations echo through the body's cells directly versus just audible.

GUIDED MEDITATION

If you are still sitting in the dark, can't find a door, can't visualize, general meditation music still isn't doing it, then go with guided meditation. Guided meditation is where another person speaks and walks you through your meditation session with music in the background. Some guided meditation is simply music based, but make sure you check the video or audio to determine what you will be experiencing. It is a little unnerving if you are listening to a waterfall and then unexpectedly some man's voice starts speaking, and you weren't expecting that.

CHANTING

Chanting is an ancient tradition done throughout the world. Certain key words have been determined to resonate at a certain frequency, so by hearing them and by saying them at a certain tone and tempo, you will begin to resonate at that frequency. Below are the chant words and what they correspond to. You will have Buddhist monks chanting in these tones.

+ OM = purifying your ego
+ MA = purifies jealousy
+ NI = purifies your passion
+ PAD = purifies ignorance
+ ME = purifies greed
+ HUM = purifies hatred

CHAPTER 28

YOGA, PILATES, REIKI, TAI CHI, AND QIGONG

YOGA AND PILATES

Yoga and Pilates are stretching and flowing energy forms of exercise that also involve breathing techniques to increase flow and move toxins out of the body. They require a calm and centered focus to perform. Yoga and Pilates have a more structural and muscular focus. This is another area where there are ample books and videos, or local shops, so go do your research and see what fits for you.

If you are physically in the state I used to be, then Yoga might be diffi-cult for you to do for a while. When I was dealing with the worst of my autoimmune dis-ease I could not hold a Yoga stretch for more than fifteen second at a time without negative consequences. Some stretches and poses actually caused me more pain than relieving it. You have to know your body and what state your body is in and then modify accordingly. If you begin a daily habit of stretching, breathing, and meditation, you will start to bring your body and spirit back in balance.

As your overall health improves, you will find your ability to do Yoga/Pilates/Tai Chi is increased. Even if you start out with two minutes of light stretching when you first wake up, it helps the blood start circulating better and moving lactic acid and other pooling toxins to cycle out. Over time, two minutes turns into five minutes, maybe eventually ten. Maybe you can only hold a stretch for five seconds, eventually, you can hold it for twenty seconds. Start slow, listen to your body, adjust accordingly. If you need to use furniture for balance, then use furniture and work up to not needing it. It is a process, but you are on the path to improving your physical situation.

Pilates is also a stretching and energy form of exercise. The main difference between Yoga and Pilates is that Yoga is used for improving the flexibility of the body and your joints. Whereas Pilates focuses on trying to relax muscles that are tense and provide strengthening for muscles of the body.

BREATHING AND RELEASING ENERGY

Breathing is an important part of releasing negative energy and improving the body. Specific breathing techniques can assist you in producing more oxygen in the bloodstream, which then turns into moving toxins out of the body. Releasing energy through breathing techniques allows for energy that is stuck to move. There are several breathing techniques you can employ but one where you incorporate steady deep breathing while you meditate will help you to open your chakras. Breathing techniques also help lower stress and anxiety.

Another area that proper breathing can assist in is sexual intercourse if you are an individual that has trouble orgasming. When you are approaching orgasm, are you breathing deeply, in and out? Or are you tense and holding your breath? If you are inhaling deeply (and pulling the sexual energy inward) and exhaling (releasing the energy) as you approach orgasm—you are likely to have well-integrated sacral energy. If you are tensed up and holding your breath as you approach orgasm, try breathing deeply and rhythmically. Often tensing is due to previous sexual trauma, so that is a shadow area for you to pursue if that is the case. Unlocking your chakras with breathing can be done if focused properly.

REIKI

Reiki is a Japanese healing technique based on the idea that someone can channel energy into or out of another person by means of touch. The goal being to activate the natural healing processes of the body and restore physical and emotional well-being. Reiki sessions have become quite popular in recent times as a healing mechanism. Reiki masters can perform these energy alignments without both people being in the same room. Remember, energy has no boundaries of time and space. My first Reiki session was with someone 1,000 miles away, and I felt the calmest I had felt in years after. In fact, I felt pretty unbothered by just about anything for two days afterward and felt like I was one with the flow.

Reiki can be performed either hands on or hands off even if both people are in the room. In a Reiki session, the therapist can physically feel which of your chakras are blocked and which are in alignment. From there, they look to move energy through the corresponding chakra so they become aligned, or at least get stuck energy moving out of the body.

QIGONG AND TAI CHI

Qigong incorporates what we learned in our yoga practice, using breath and qi to move and unblock stuck energy and ultimately begin to heal the body through learning how to move and receive energy. It has been part of Chinese culture going back 4,000 years. Qigong typically involves moving meditation, coordinating slow-flowing movement, deep rhythmic breathing, and a calm meditative state of mind. People practice qigong for recreation, exercise, relaxation, preventive medicine, self-healing, meditation, and training for martial arts.

Tai Chi is a Chinese martial art practiced for defense training, health benefits, and meditation done through a series of slow-movement physical exercises and stretches. Each posture flows into the next without pause, ensuring that your body is in constant motion through gentle movements which connect the mind and body.

What is the difference between tai chi and qigong? Qigong can be thought of as a movement you do for a certain situation, whereas tai chi is a series of movements that work on the entire body in a flowing sequence.

CHAPTER 29

ALCHEMY

Alchemy is a topic I struggled with as in the practical application of it in today's world. There are energy alchemists who are healers that transmute negative lower vibrational energy into positive higher vibrational energy. This is why you see some energy healers note themselves as Alchemists. The difference between a regular energy healer and an energy Alchemist is that an Alchemist is strong enough to maintain their energy field without disruption from other's fields and then is able to transmute the problem energy into a positive way that does not do harm to self or others. Whereas a regular energy healer is more about simply moving that energy to a different space out of the body and aligning the chakras.

I understood this practice when I went to do some energy healing on my son. I had cleared my energy field and felt pretty good for about a week and was expecting some form of psychic attack. But none seemed to come, except my son started complaining of odd pains several days in a row. He would wake up, and he said it felt like someone had been punching his stomach and his stomach was sore. He felt icky. I wondered if, in my protection of self, I had forgotten to do protection for my child. As he laid down and I sat with him, I made a critical error. I forgot to clear and hold my energy shield before I started my healing. I worked on gently pulling out the toxic energy, but I didn't capture and contain the energy and convert it properly. Within seconds of me finishing, I felt a horrible sickness. It did not feel like a normal sickness. It was so bad I had to immediately lie down until I had enough energy to sit up and clear my field. Lesson learned. An alchemist can take energy from, say a cancer patient, and transmute that and use it to then heal without taking on the toxic energy from the cancer.

More tangible Alchemy is aligned to ancient alchemy, which really is the first metallurgists and chemists. Ancient alchemy is typically identified with understanding the principles of metallurgy at its most basic level, through understanding how one uses the seven metals of alchemy in conjunction with the Platonic solids and elements. It is a combination of sacred geometry, chemistry, mathematics, and science all combined in their work. There are seven metals used in ancient alchemy that are considered properties that make all other possibilities: gold, silver, mercury, copper, iron, tin, and lead.

There are people who are shamans, energy alchemists, reiki energy healers, all who do fascinating things that move energy, remove dis-eases, and can completely change your body. There are some who don't, but the ones you are looking for are the women aged fifty to eighty who have been doing this weird stuff for thirty-plus years. They know stuff that doesn't make sense, seems weird, but works. I go into any session with one of these women with a completely open and undoubting mind. Yes, this woman is going to do whatever she says she is capable of doing for me, and I am going to lean into that, and then we will just see how that plays out. If you enter any session for healing with doubt, then you are blocking the energy flow and the healing process. In short, you are blocking the healer. Then you wonder why the healing didn't have quite the effect it did. Or maybe you got lucky, and it did, and you were left shocked and pondering the secrets of the universe again.

CHAPTER 30

LIGHT CODES

If you see shapes or colors in meditation, you may be receiving light codes. Everything emits an energy pattern, even words. Light codes are energy patterns that all of creation emits, and within them is encoded healing energy, thoughts, and imprinted emotions. Basically, light codes are symbols that hold energy. When put together in a series, they are called a light language. When we connect with that energy, we become the channel for it, we allow that energy to move through our body then out through our hands into our codes or out through our voice if we speak light language.

Light codes manifest in energy patterns, sacred geometry, colors, sound waves, light patterns, and frequencies that all living things radiate. We are able to access those transmissions through light language as one modality. Every living being is encoded at birth with a specific set of codes that they are to transmit during their lifetime. While light codes might not make sense to the normal conscious mind, they will indeed be perceived, understood, and acknowledged by your higher self or oversoul.

Some people carry light codes from higher realms or galactic origins and are able to activate them in others. Some will simply write them out, and others will sign with their hands. Lots of people are seeing various light code transmissions at this time, and you can find videos of them online. When someone signs light codes, the energy from their hands is transferred to the person/object they are working on, much like giving an energy healing.

CHAPTER 31

DIET AND THE
PHYSICAL BODY

I never thought I would be able to go vegetarian. I still am not quite there, but I am close. Most of the meat I eat these days is plant-based protein, aka fake meat. In the journey to eating better, you find out some information about our food sources that is disturbing. The gluten issue is due to genetic modification of the gluten in wheat crops. Most of our water supply is polluted or chemically altered. Even over time, small amounts of trace toxins build up to chemically alter the cellular structure of our bodies. Mostly due to the containers our food and drinks are stored in (plastics).

We also know that the mind and the gut are linked and critical to the body's physical health. I've read that the human body is actually designed to live 120–125 years at its longest life. Now think about what we do to our bodies that decreases the ability for us to do that. The air we breathe is polluted, the water we drink is poisoned, and the soil we get our food source from is also poisoned and dying.

Did you know that red cabbage and red grapes are high in anti-cancer properties? Why doesn't western medicine have as part of the healing process diet changes for cancer patients? CBD Oil also has cancer-fighting properties, and yet for so many years, the government and corporations were so opposed to natural occurring remedies as a way to heal. Because that doesn't put money into the health care industry if we heal people. You also have a harder time controlling the population levels with a healthier populace.

Antioxidants help to neutralize free radicals that can cause cellular and DNA damage. Ginger, curcumin, and turmeric are great for reducing inflammation, along with a lot of other vegetables like cucumbers. We discussed in the grounding section that the root cause of all dis-eases is a damaged cell. Emotional traumas activate the disease, but the physical breakdown is that a cell is inflamed or damaged. So you need to work on how to fix the inflammation properties of your cells through your diet as well by eating foods that cater to anti-inflammation.

Depending on your specific dis-ease, I suggest looking into a holistic nutritionist. Changes in diet alone have shown to eradicate diseases and bring significant relief in pain. Local fruits and vegetables can make a huge difference. Switching out processed sugar for local honey is another way to make changes in the type of sugar intake.

I took these things, some for improved health and for heavy metal detox: Turmeric, Krill Oil, Sea Moss (capsules), Chlorophyll (capsules), CBD Oil, sea cucumber (capsules), Vitamin D, and a concoction of lemon/lime/cucumber/ginger/pineapple/cranberry or pomegranate juice)

ALKALINE WATER

There is a lot to relearn about the benefits of our food. I suggest finding alkaline shops online for more information or picking up some books on alkaline diets. When I first went down the water route in researching diet, one of the things it directly led me to was the fluoride in the water controversial topic. I remember thinking the fluoride conspiracy theory was a bit out there. But I never did any research on it until now, and what I found astounded me. Fluoride is one of the main active ingredients in rat poison. It is classified as a poison by the FDA. Fluoride also happens to calcify the pineal gland. So your third eye might have restrictions simply because of the calcification build-up in your pineal gland. Seriously do your research on fluoride in water, and you will walk away with a different viewpoint.

Understand that your tap water and toothpaste has fluoride in it. So the solution is to drink alkaline water and switch to fluoride-free toothpaste. You can pick some up in your local grocery store or you can make your own toothpaste with natural ingredients. Humans' current eating habits lean the human body to be on the acidic side of the scale. Diabetes even causes your blood to turn acidic. You can start to counter that by drinking alkaline water, which means it is rich in calcium, silica, potassium, magnesium, and bicarbonate. Alkalizing restores pH balance by reducing acidity levels in the body.

If you can balance your body's pH to be alkaline, then you can starve the dis-eased cells from thriving. Again, I highly recommend seeing a holistic nutritionist and a functional doctor. They will be able to craft a plan to assist you in restructuring your diet based on your body's needs.

EPIGENETICS

Epigenetics is the study of heritable changes in gene expression that do not involve changes to the underlying DNA sequence. In short, it is about measuring changes that happened in previous generations and how that translates down the gene pool. Let me tell you about a scenario that explains epigenetics.

Scientists put five monkeys in a room with a bunch of bananas and a rope to climb to get to it. One of the monkeys climbs the rope, at which point it gets sprayed with cold water as do the other monkeys. They sit there cold, wet, and hungry. But another monkey decides to be brave and climb the rope. Again it and all the other monkeys get sprayed with cold water. A third monkey attempts, and the other monkeys, not wanting to be sprayed, pull him off and beat him. One monkey is removed, and a new monkey is introduced to the group. The new monkey sees the bananas and goes for it. But the rest of the monkeys pull him down and beat him. One original monkey is removed and a new monkey introduced. Same thing happens. This continues until there are no original monkeys. At this point, when a new monkey is introduced, it has no idea why it is getting beat.

Same is true for much of human history. We don't know why we continue to do the same things other than … it is tradition.

CHAPTER 32

THE PATH FORWARD

We have thought for centuries that IF intelligent life does exist in the universe or other universes, they aren't more technologically advanced or they would have found us first. But really, we say that as if they haven't, and the technology they are using doesn't contain cloaking technology using energy that is harnessed to continuously power their ships without contaminants ruining the atmosphere. The evidence is out there that they exist. So far, the ones we have seen haven't harmed us. Unless you count the alien abductions in the 70s and 80s. Even the reasons behind alien abductions are not clear if the intent was to harm us or if your soul agreed to be abducted for research before you came into the human plane. If you take Cannon's work on alien abductions, the subjects all recount memories from their abductions that differ from their conscious recollections. In them, they note they had previously agreed before they came into Earth to be one of the people who agree to be abducted for research purposes. And the methods used aren't as awful as they thought.

Are they really among us peacefully? Are they controlling us somehow? It is a little unclear at this time. There was a clip in the movie *Close Encounters of the Fifth* Kind where Dr. Greer was talking about an incident that happened when Bush Sr was president, and a group of politicians were going to officially expose that aliens are among us. One of the leaders was abducted right out of his car. Others were told by whoever these alien abductors were that if they moved forward with it, they would abduct all world leaders. So they abandoned the plan. Could this be why we don't have disclosure even though the emperor has no clothes? Possibly. It certainly makes me think if that was the directive, then they aren't working in our (humans) best interest. Observation under secrecy could mean a few things. It could mean we are looked at like a zoo or a science experiment. Let's be honest, if they wanted to wipe us out, they could easily do so.

Is it really a stretch to say that maybe a lot of the sci-if story plot lines in books and movies are really just a type of telepathic ability by their creators that accessed past memories in their consciousness or tapping into the collective consciousness to find an event that really did occur, just elsewhere? It is extremely common for two or three people in the world to be creating the same song, a book, or a science experiment at the same time. Are they really creating something original? Or are they tapping into a higher consciousness of a repeated previous event and repeating it in the now? Are the people in question who have no real connection, tapping into the same creative consciousness at the same time? And if abilities like this exist, then is it so hard to believe that ET's also have more advanced psychic abilities? And if they do have more psychic abilities, maybe metaphysics is an area that needs to be given more serious thought.

While having a conversation with someone, have you ever thought you could hear their thoughts? But then what they say seems to slightly counter them? And your gut tells you something is off? Do you brush it off as taking them for their word, or do you use that as a piece of information to say, "Seems there might be dishonesty?" Then some time down the line, you find some other information that indicates that person is less than trustworthy? That is using your gut. Your instinct. Your intuition. Your energetic forcefield. Your connected consciousness. Which is another way of saying, you are using some psychic connection to make an assertion.

We have been playing out this reincarnation and ascension scene over and over for thousands of years. Each time we come back in, forgetting the levels we cleared previously. But how is that helpful? Murders, rapes, abuse, trauma. The psychological trauma and its impacts on the vessel of this species, the human body.

We choose not to live in symbiosis with the Earth but instead destroy it and punting our generational problems to the next generation to deal with. We further cause problems in how we grow our food. What we are doing to the soil or not doing to the soil. Same for the air we breathe and water we use. How we package and ship our food. I recently read an article that mentioned we ingest through the drinks in plastic bottles, the food packaging rub off (plastic), and when we heat our food in plastic—approximately five grams of plastic or the equivalent of a credit card each week. Now imagine that the particles are getting deposited in your organs. Even worse, doing detoxes doesn't mean you are necessarily able to remove that. We have more cancer and diseases in the last seventy years than we ever have had.

In the last thirty years, we have mentally sped up our thought processes and exposure to external stimuli due to the technological advancements in creating the internet, voice communication, and social interaction for billions of individuals. Our minds are processing data at an exponential rate. While the financial component of who makes the money and thus who makes the rules has switched from one of either royal bloodline name or a conquered to a pure … capitalist concept, it really is the same underlying problem all along. All that happened was the team who was in charge changed.

Be careful as you are learning in your journey. Both with yourself and others you are involving in your process. Careful of the massive amount of people that are just not where you are, nor even want to consider a different lens to look through than what they know. Their perception may shift to, this person is having a psychotic break. You will learn pretty quickly who you can and cannot have conversations with. I have learned to use some key words or phrases which quickly identify the situation. You will figure out what those are for you.

The spiritual shifts, while confusing and scary, represent a change in one's core belief systems. As a result, the people around you, who love and care for you who are NOT going through this shift with you, all they see is erratic behavior and their loved one talking about shit that sounds off the wall. At that point, you are only a few steps away from either alienating family and friends or having a psychological intervention by them. This is hard for many people. Your core belief structure changing is hard enough, but for them, it's kind of like saying, I know we have been Catholic for my whole life, but I just really feel like I should be Mormon now and move to Utah. When you explain something they don't believe happens, because it doesn't to them, or they have never witnessed it or wanted to believe, or they specifically say that is not possible, just let it go. You are trying to get them to validate something that is just not tangible to them. It just isn't their time.

My advice is to let it go. Find the community where you feel welcome, whether it is locally or online. Maintain your current relationships to the best of your ability as they have been established previously unless you realize you are better off releasing them. If you find one of your friends or family is at least open to you talking to them simply as an outlet for you, then use it. I have a couple of friends that, while they aren't where I am, are still open to me at least discussing what I am going through and learning because it is interesting to them and because they love me enough to be open in that way.

Do your own timeline reviews of your past experiences and see what you connect. When I went through the discovery of being an empath my brain mentally exploded that instead of the terms: oh she is just high energy, wired, emotional, all over the map, probably has anxiety, that in fact, I was an empath. One who has been operating unaware of it, and as a result, has no idea how to manage it properly to my advantage and others. From there, I went back in my timeline on the empath information to all of the consistent comments that were made. The feelings I always had, the energy, the weirdness, it was like … oh my God! A total mind-splitting moment and a shift. Everything coming together in a way that made sense, and again, others were too. As if your life path had only been viewed from ground level, and then one day, you see a topical view.

There will be many things you will want to do your own timeline reviews with. Once you start to explore them, your brain then starts shifting the data into a pattern based on the new information in your mind and how the energy of your body aligns with that data, and then it maps it together, and you see how all these pieces that seemed random or traits where "this just is who I am," have a ton of more structure, understanding, and clarity. When that happens, it is like … whoa. It is okay to pause after doing these timeline reviews to reflect and give yourself the emotional and mental headspace to process things you are discovering.

Understand that as you go on this path and as you meet people in the spiritual community, there are dishonest and disingenuous scammers in our community too. People pretending to be Lightworkers when they are not, people taking advantage of vulnerable people looking for help. This is where your intuition is key. If you come up against someone you are like—I am not sure this one is part of the pack. Well, you probably are right then. In fact, it is the more experienced intuitives who were the ones that warned me about this. There are people who claim to have gifts or see things or hear things, but don't.

I wanted a lot of people to just … JUST GIVE ME THE ANSWERS STRAIGHT! I hate to say it, and it will take you diving into yourself to understand what I mean, but that's not how it works. What I found is that when I stopped wanting someone else to give me ALL the answers, I started realizing that everyone was giving me a clue, or sometimes several clues. I needed to follow the clues myself and piece my own puzzle together. You will need to do the same. Don't be afraid to lean on the gifts of others to help you do that. We all have a role to play, but it also has to play itself out and in conjunction with others. You will see a lot of people say, simply go within. All the answers are inside you. That is both accurate and not accurate. Because in the beginning, if you only do that, it's pretty much like driving your car but never getting out of the parking lot. Or hopping on the merry-go-round by yourself and never getting off. Once you have figured more things out by getting your clues, then you start doing more inward dives to process what you have found.

As you are researching online, you will find people and articles that say, social media and technology is evil, and you need to completely disconnect. To some degree yes. But the truth is, if we didn't have online technology, we would not be connecting at the rate we currently are with each other. We would not be finding each other nor the information that exists by others who are sharing.

I love the internet. I find information, read it, and say—okay how did I feel about that? What is the viability of that? How does that play into what I already know or have connected or is it the missing piece to something

I have been looking for? Some of it I am like, well that sounds like crap, or that sounds a little too light and airy for me, or I found a new piece of mind-blowing information I did not think I was going to discover and now need to step back and process all of that. Or it could be you are reading or watching something, and they had you all the way up to the end and then threw something out there that you were like, okay that might be one step too far, and I definitely think you took a hard right there.

Like anything, there is information that seems legit or makes sense, and then there is some misinformation out there. Start kicking up your bullshit meter to figure out which is which. Don't blindly believe something just because you are new to this and someone wrote something articulately. You may read something that makes you go, that totally makes sense, and I can buy into that theory, even if it does not personally resonate with you. If you find yourself with a piece of information that either is in conflict with something, or you aren't sure where it fits, put it on a shelf in your mind to circle back to at a later time when you find some new piece of information that connects it, or completely refutes it.

When dealing with a human that someone puts up on a pedestal as an enlightened being, an ascended master, someone working for "the light," ask yourself this one question. Does this person and the words they say and the actions they do, represent someone who has compassion, empathy, and the collective good of all and any humans at the forefront of what they do? Or do they sow division, chaos, and whose past and current actions have been hateful, hurtful, and egoistic? Is it all about them and what they can achieve or gain, or is it about humans as a collective and the growth and progressive evolution of us all?

Our consciousness has come from somewhere else. Each Starseed has a mission on Earth, specifically in this lifetime more than previous ones. All of our missions, however, have the same theme running through them—to elevate the collective consciousness from a polarity driven concept to one of harmony and unity. In doing so, each of us has a role to play in expanding others' understanding of higher levels of consciousness and to get us out of this power-driven, physical suppression, and oppression of people en masse, including degradation of females. It is to drive out fear and expose untruths to others, so they expand their conscious thinking patterns.

I once saw a video on YouTube which I can't find now but this scene they built out about Awakening, is a good synopsis of the process.

Picture yourself as a member of your cosmic identity, not human one. You are much larger than your human form. Visualize being in a classroom, and an instructor is telling you about the system you will enter, so you are aware of what to expect as part of this assignment.

You are at the top of your profession. You believe you are an impeccable systems buster and are reconstructors of reality. The professor is telling you when you go down to Earth. You will need us to come and instruct and help you because you won't remember any of this. You laugh because as cool and arrogant as you are now, you know once you go through the veil, you won't remember any of this. But you still will think you will.

Watch this, he says, we will show you pictures. Here, see you are in a vehicle, and we are coming through, and you act as if you don't understand what is going on in your human disguise. This is part of your assignment, you are briefed on all of this, and you understand.

If you knew as much as your higher self does at this time, you would be very impatient with this assignment. I mean, imagine your cosmic self as a human, thinking as a human, evolving yourself into something higher than a human, only to then realize you were more than a human all along. But you still have to go through the process to evolve. Sometimes we have made some stuff up along the way in order to activate something in you in order for you to grow. We are very crafty teachers.

LET'S RECAP

+ Everything is composed of energy and vibrates at different frequencies.
+ Governments and religious organizations do not and never have had the best interests of the people in the forefront. Your history of humanity has been hidden and disguised and misinformation mixed in with the real information put out by those in power and authority to suit their agendas and narrative.
+ The God as defined in monotheistic religions is not accurate, nor the idea you only live one life.
+ Religion is a control mechanism to isolate you from your own divinity and shame you into believing you aren't worthy and are born a sinner. It restricts your spirituality instead of aligning you to your connectedness to Source and the collective consciousness of all things.
+ Money is a slave system designed to keep the masses of people in lower states of fear, shame, depression, anxiety, and sadness.
+ Politics and race are geographical boundaries that are a control system meant to further divide people and pit them against each other.
+ Your air, water, and food sources have been poisoned.
+ You can heal yourself, as the human body is designed to.
+ You need to alter your diet and drink alkaline water.
+ Do your shadow work and release your traumas, forgive and sit in acceptance and self-love.
+ Meditate, ground and center yourself, and raise your vibrational frequency.
+ Don't allow anyone to challenge your version of reality no matter how weird it is.

✦ Anyone who sits in a place of sowing chaos, division, anger, hate, self-centered ideologies is not "part of the light team's plan" and is not to be trusted. Use your discernment.

✦ Redirect your focus to the service of others in this transformative journey and away from service only to self (ego).

✦ You can raise the vibrational frequency of the Earth and the collective consciousness to change the trajectory of our current path.

✦ Fight for the rights of ALL people back, in whatever way that calls to you.

Good luck on your journey! I have faith in you.

ABOUT THE
AUTHOR

It doesn't matter who I am. What I have or haven't done.
All that matters is what you're going to do with
the information I gave you.

Made in the USA
Las Vegas, NV
19 December 2021

38814891R00168